WORD POLITICS

Verbal Strategy Among the Superpowers

PREPARED UNDER THE AUSPICES OF
THE CENTER FOR INTERNATIONAL STUDIES
NEW YORK UNIVERSITY

NEW YORK UNIVERSITY
CENTER FOR INTERNATIONAL STUDIES
Studies in Peaceful Change

Why Federations Fail: An Inquiry into the Requisites for Successful Federalism, Thomas M. Franck, Gisbert H. Flanz, Herbert J. Spiro, and Frank N. Trager (New York: New York University Press), 1968

A Free Trade Association, Thomas M. Franck and Edward Weisband, eds. (New York: New York University Press), 1968

Comparative Constitutional Process, Thomas M. Franck (New York: Praeger; London: Sweet and Maxwell), 1968

The Structure of Impartiality, Thomas M. Franck (New York: Macmillan), 1968

Agents of Change: A Close Look at the Peace Corps, David Hapgood and Meridan Bennett (Boston: Little, Brown), 1968

Law, Reason and Justice: Essays in Legal Philosophy, Graham B. Hughes (New York: New York University Press), 1969

Czechoslovakia: Intervention and Impact, I. William Zartman, ed. (New York: New York University Press), 1970

Sierra Leone: An Experiment in Democracy in an African Nation, Gershon Collier (New York: New York University Press), 1970

Microstates and Micronesia: Problems of America's Pacific Islands and Other Minute Territories, Stanley A. de Smith (New York: New York University Press), 1970

International Business Negotiations: A Study in India, Ashok Kapoor (New York: New York University Press), 1970

Foreign Capital for Economic Development: A Korean Case Study, Seung Hee Kim (New York: Praeger), 1970

The Politics of Trade Negotiations Between Africa and the European Economic Community: The Weak Confront the Strong, I. William Zartman (Princeton, New Jersey: Princeton University Press), 1971

WORD POLITICS

Verbal Strategy
Among the Superpowers

THOMAS M. FRANCK
EDWARD WEISBAND

New York   OXFORD UNIVERSITY PRESS   *1971*

To Jan Palach
and the people everywhere who
   cared about the Prague spring

Preface

When United States forces invaded the Dominican Republic, Washington arrogantly confronted the Organization of American States with a *fait accompli* more of the era of 1865 than 1965. But when the Warsaw Pact Powers brutally and stupidly suppressed Alexander Dubcek's attempt to impose a human face on socialism, the West was stunned and horrified. Few Western observers noted that the Russians were echoing the very words used by hardheaded realists in Washington to defend America's Latin American policy. By failing to listen to themselves as if they were the enemy speaking, American policy makers had made it easy and cheap for Russia to reassert the darkest side of its nature. This cannot but be counted a failure of U.S. strategic planning.

It is easy to show that a national security policy is wrong once one rejects national security assumptions. We, however, have tried to show that even by the very system of strategic accounting used by the national-interest brokers, the United States has been playing a losing game. The hardheaded realists in the White House and State Department, not just Dubcek, were the real losers when Soviet tanks entered Prague. And to some extent, these Western losses were self-inflicted.

We believe we have been able to show this without moralizing or resorting to subjective emotionalism. Our method is to compare the concepts which United States strategists developed vis-à-vis Guatemala, Cuba, and the Dominican Republic with those Soviet leaders developed vis-à-vis Hungary and Czechoslovakia, and to indicate how concepts affect strategic cost in super-power politics.

We do not assert that what we did in relation to our small neighbors is as bad as what the Russians did in relation to theirs.

We do not assert that our action in the Dominican Republic is the operative cause of the Soviet suppression of Czechoslovakia. Causality is far more complex; there were many intervening variables—the most important, one might guess, was our evident pre-occupation with Vietnam.

But we do show that the ways we chose to conceptualize our national and regional rights and privileges in the Western Hemisphere are precisely indistinguishable from those most recently given prominence by the Soviet Union in the Brezhnev Doctrine. We show that Russia and its Warsaw Pact "family" were able to provide logically and legally impeccable cover for the brutalization of Czechoslovakia without stepping one word or phrase beyond the conceptual parameters the United States and, at our urging, the Organization of American States had devised, expressed, and put into practice between 1953 and 1965.

We believe that this single, provable fact is of real strategic and systemic importance. We show that it represents poor strategy and an important cost to our national interest. We show that it handed an important benefit to the Soviet Union.

At one level, this book is for strategists, for it shows how ill-conceived concepts come back as charges against the national interest. We say things which, in the long run, are counter to our interest. And we say these things to cover actions which trade doubtful short-term gains for predictable but unanticipated long-term costs: costs to our strategic credibility, costs to our world image, costs to the international system in which we have an extremely important share.

At a somewhat different level, we have deliberately chosen to proceed with systemic rather than ethical or idealistic analysis because we believe that in so doing we are able to show that an amorally conceived foreign policy, at least for the United States,

is likely also to be unsuccessful by the standards of "hard" strategy
and national-interest cost/benefit accounting. We intend that some
readers conclude that any action by the United States which cannot be credibly set out in terms that build and strengthen a conceptual framework for the kind of reciprocally principled world
we want, can never be in our national interest. This is what we aim
to show in Chapter 8. It is at the systemic level of understanding
strategy that strategy and morality, so long set apart in the name
of hardheaded realism, can be seen to be sides of the same coin.

At its most fundamental level, then, this study proposes a new
and, we urge, far more realistic system of strategic cost-accounting
than has previously been used by the hardheaded realists in Washington. We believe that actions based on concepts that make the
United States and the Soviet Union appear to share a lowest common denominator of behavior in foreign policy, a common disregard for sovereignty, diversity, and peace, is much costlier to
the United States than to the Soviet Union. We believe that every
time "we" play by "their" rules, we incur a long-term cost that
outweighs any short-term gain.

In developing these themes, we benefited from the advice
and reactions of numerous people. High on the list of those who
tempered our efforts with wise counsel is Richard N. Gardner,
Professor of Law and International Relations at Columbia University who served as Deputy Assistant Secretary of State for International Organization Affairs from 1961 to 1965. Professor Roger
Hilsman of Columbia University, who also served as an Assistant
Secretary of State in the Kennedy Administration, contributed his
unique understanding of the politics of policy making in a series
of critical comments of an earlier draft.

The Honorable U. Haluk Bayulken, Ambassador and Chief
Representative, Permanent Mission of Turkey to the United Nations, the Honorable Yvon Beaulne, Ambassador and Chief Representative, Permanent Mission of Canada to the United Nations,
both elucidated this study with suggestions based on experiences
growing out of years of public service, as did two particularly

knowledgeable members of the United Kingdom Mission to the U.N., Miss Sheila Hardin and Mrs. Beryl Chitty. The Honorable Seymour M. Finger, Ambassador, United States Mission to the United Nations, although he disagreed with parts of our text, made a number of useful comments which we have incorporated. So, too, did Mrs. Marietta Tree who drew our attention to certain important historical parallels.

Professor Edmund O. Stillman, of the Hudson Institute and The Johns Hopkins University, advised us to focus on strategy and avoid moral issues—advice we have tried to follow for the reasons stated above. The Honorable Thomas C. Mann, who played a key role in many of the crises we discuss, without in any way violating his trust, provided us with invaluable insights into the historic parallels, the options, and the human dilemmas faced by Presidents Kennedy and Johnson. In particular, Mr. Mann made a case for the position that President Johnson's speech of May 2, 1965, was intended to restate a gradually evolved hemispheric doctrine and not to initiate a new one: particularly not one seeking to establish a generalized U.S. right to intervene with military force against any Marxist government anywhere in the hemisphere.

Our appreciation goes particularly to Professor Louis B. Sohn who read earlier drafts of parts of this manuscript and made detailed substantive and editorial suggestions for almost every page. These were absolutely invaluable. A very helpful earlier reading was also given, with customary humor and a sharp editorial eye for the irrelevant, by Miss Judy Friedlaender.

Professor Harold Guetzkow was extraordinarily generous in giving us some of that most precious of the scholar's commodities—his year's leave of absence—to help us turn some of the ideas arising out of this book into game-testable hypotheses. Mr. David Bronheim, Executive Director, Center for Inter-American Relations, allowed us to benefit from his exceptional grasp of Latin American history. He also urged us to distinguish between

American policy toward Central America and toward the rest of the Hemisphere.

Our appreciation also goes to two outstanding students of international law, Professor Tom Farer of the Columbia University School of Law and Professor Gidon Gottlieb, School of Law, New York University, who examined the legal aspects of our argument with the care, insight, and imagination for which they are properly known. Mr. Raymond S. Rubinow also made helpful suggestions.

Most important, we wish to acknowledge the great debt owed the Junior and Senior Fellows of the Center for International Studies. Over the past three years they have created an environment truly conducive to an inter-disciplinary policy-oriented study such as this. During two colloquia held at the Center, they devoted themselves to ways of strengthening the text. It is in no way meant as a mere platitude to say that the book in its present form would not have been possible without them. In this regard, special mention should be made of Morris J. Blachman, a Junior Fellow of the Center 1967–69, and at present completing his Ph.D. dissertation in the Department of Politics of New York University.

S. M. Miller, Professor of Educational Sociology, School of Education, New York University, and Mr. Roy Bennett, U.N. correspondent of the London *Tribune,* who are working jointly on a study of the Cold War and imperialism as Senior Fellows of the Center, as well as Mr. William A. Douglas, Country Program Director for Peru, American Institute for Free Labor, who has completed a study of political institutions in Latin America as a Senior Fellow also deserve special thanks for having added certain deepening insights.

We have been fortunate in having three highly competent and dedicated Research Associates at the Center during the three academic years of work on this project. Mr. Kenneth Gold gathered and compiled much of the documentation used here to illustrate U.S. verbal strategy toward Latin America between the years 1954 and 1965. Thanks also go to his successors, Mr. John C. Bender, presently the Assistant Director of the Center, and Mr. Nigel Rodley, Research Associate at the Center during the current academic year, both of whom were helpful in supplemental data gathering. Mr. Bender also helped significantly to edit an earlier draft of what was to be one chapter of this book; it appeared in the *American Journal of International Law,* and we then decided that it had been sufficiently exposed. It is, thus, not included here.

Miss Jane Friedlaender filled the margins of an early draft manuscript with the sorts of notes that one appreciates from very close friends. Hopefully, a more literate style has emerged that does not mark us with the lawyer's and political scientist's stigma.

Our deepest appreciation goes to Mrs. Donna Welensky and Mrs. Phyllis B. Goldberg. Mrs. Welensky typed the first version of this study and continued to help throughout. Mrs. Goldberg typed the several succeeding versions and became an experienced cryptographer in the process. She also checked footnotes and helped with useful stylistic and other suggestions. In many ways this book owes its completion to her sense of personal involvement and felicitous care.

The Law Center Foundation provided the financial support that allowed us to work on this project for three months in the summer of 1969, liberated from our time-devouring office routines.

Invaluable, too, were the unflagging encouragements of Dean Robert B. McKay and Dean Bert S. Prunty of the New York University Law Faculty, and the Faculty Colloquium of the N.Y.U. Department of Politics, chaired by Professor I. William Zartman. We also appreciated the forum for testing our ideas provided by the Columbia University Seminar on the Problems of Peace, and its distinguished chairman, Professor John N. Hazard.

Authors, tired and blinded by overexposure to their written and rewritten words, are seldom able to discern the point at which an embryonic manuscript has at last matured into a completed text. A trusted and distinguished colleague can sometimes do this for them. In our case, we were most fortunate to have such a colleague in Professor Stanley Hoffmann.

In no way are any of the above to be held responsible for the views expressed or for the limitations and defects found herein, which are entirely our own.

T. M. F.
E. W.

New York City
April 1971

Contents

WORD POLITICS

Verbal Strategy Among the Superpowers

". . . the rhetoric in international affairs does make a difference."

President Richard M. Nixon
January 4, 1971

1

Verbal Behavior, System Transformation, and Crisis Management

In August 1968 the Soviet Union and its Warsaw Pact allies invaded Czechoslovakia. This raising of the arm by socialist brother against brother was all the more extraordinary because troops from neighboring Peoples' Democracies, states still at the first stop along the road to communism, were used to suppress a country which had already reached the advanced stage of a socialist republic. It was as if bishops had unseated a cardinal.

Extraordinary, too, was the insensitive use of German (GDR) troops, in the name of socialist unity, on the thirtieth anniversary of the Nazi conquest of Czechoslovakia in the name of Pan-Teutonic solidarity.

Most shocking of all, however, was the seeming instability and erraticism that the Czechoslovak adventure gave the Soviet leadership. Men who had come to be widely regarded in the West as stable, responsible technocrats were suddenly looked at again, and now seemed dangerously idiosyncratic and unpredictable. The Czechoslovak invasion stood out in grotesque contrast to the pattern of Soviet behavior that the West had come to regard as normative. The Kremlin leaders had made their peace with Tito, ratified the sovereign equality of all socialist states, stopped short of burying the once unorthodox Gomulka, proclaimed the existence of different roads to socialism, and tolerated Romanian neutralism in both the great rift with China and the campaign against Israel. The suppressions of East German and Hungarian self-assertiveness had receded into a crude past, the frontier days of socialism's postwar expansion westward.

The Czechoslovak invasion thus upset the euphoric view (shared—with some exceptions—in Washington, Belgrade, Paris, and Prague during the mid-1960's) that the new age of super-power *détente* had, indeed, as the late President Kennedy had predicted, achieved a loosening of the ties constraining Russia's client states. The *détente,* moreover, had a certain balanced fairness. In return for the United States's having to put up with President De Gaulle's and Chancellor Kiesinger's obduracy, Russia had had to learn to live with Ceaucescu, Tito, and Dubcek.

But a moment came, in August 1968, when the men in the Kremlin decided that they did not have to live with Dubcek. This must have been a major decision. Evidence strongly suggests that it was arrived at reluctantly, hesitatingly, and without unanimity. One aspect of the Soviet leaders' decision, however, was simple enough: they were in no doubt about the possibility of a meaningful counteraction by the United States. No U.S. attempt was made to deter the Soviets and their allies, either by specifying a willingness to protect Czechoslovakia or by leaving our response to an invasion in any real doubt. The Russians, observing and evaluating us, had every reason to know that we would do nothing.[1]

In the summer of 1968, the United States had, as a result

---

1. In the period immediately preceding the Soviet invasion, there were many reports, never denied, that the U.S. government would "stay on the sidelines." Cf., *The New York Times,* July 22, 1968, p. 4, citing Secretary of State Rusk.

of its own policies prior to that point, lost the option to deter the invasion of Czechoslovakia. While U.S. strength in West Germany, from a purely *military-logistical* point of view, could have provided a credible negative factor in Soviet calculations, the lack of *psychological* credibility would have posed virtually insuperable problems for the U.S. Even had we wanted, it would have been difficult, at short notice, to make it clearly credible that we were ready to use the force necessary to save Czechoslovakia. This psychological component of deterrence strategy, as we shall see, is of an order of importance approximating that of armies and weapons.

It is in this connection that an understanding of the dynamics of system transformation and crisis management is essential. The Soviets were embarking on an initiative that had the considerable strategic disadvantage for them of being radically inconsistent with their own principles, professed during the de-Stalinization era, and with what both their allies and opponents had been led to expect of them in the years of reform after the Hungarian invasion. Their course of conduct thus incurred the cost of making them appear—both to opponents and to the world at large—inconsistent and erratic. Such conduct is likely to be costly, both in lost prestige among friendly and neutral states and in the danger that results from taking disequilibrating actions in a delicately poised system of interstate relations. That these potential costs of the Czechoslovak invasion were lower than they otherwise might have been is due, in a significant measure, to the prior conduct of the United States toward states in its own equivalent self-designated zone of supremacy: Latin America, the Central American and Caribbean areas in particular.

The Soviet leaders were undoubtedly aware of this. By the time the Warsaw Pact armies were being committed to the invasion, a set of principles, later known as the Brezhnev Doctrine, had been devised by Soviet strategists to justify their initiative. Even as the troops marched, these principles were being communicated to the West. In substance, they asserted that

Czechoslovakia, being a "Communist" state in the East European "commonwealth," was subject to the norms and discipline of the regional grouping. The United States had previously established the very same principles, particularly in the Johnson Doctrine, as the basis of its relations with the states of our "commonwealth"—the Western hemisphere. The Brezhnev Doctrine faithfully echoes official U.S. pronouncements made during the covert overthrow of the government of Guatemala, the Cuban missile crisis, and the invasion of the Dominican Republic. Thus the Soviets were able to claim, credibly, that the principles upon which they were acting were those we ourselves had devised to justify our conduct in the Americas, and that by our rhetoric we had implicitly signaled our consent to their application in the case of Czechoslovakia.

The Johnson and Brezhnev doctrines are virtually identical. The importance of this far transcends the issues in the Czechoslovak crisis and goes directly to the heart of national strategy. The Johnson Doctrine and the Brezhnev Doctrine are both enunciated principles. When a superpower sets out to explain its conduct to another superpower, and to the world in general, it engages in verbal strategy, that is, it seeks to locate its conduct in the context of principles that will advance the national interest. Effective verbal strategy demands not only that the principles enunciated help to achieve the immediate object of current actions but also that they do not later redound against the longer-term interest of the enunciator. To this end, certain points should be kept in mind. One is that conduct explained by principles inconsistent with those applied previously in similar circumstances, tends to transform the system. This means that the other superpower in the future will expect to have recourse to the same principles. A second point is that an action explained by a principle inconsistent with prior conduct is likely to cost the actor in prestige among other states, not only because consistency is a part of everyone's definition of justice but also because all states have a stake in the stability of the system above and beyond their stake in a particular issue confronting the system. This, again, is particularly true of relations between the superpowers where nonsystemic, idiosyncratic conduct vastly increases the prospects of a universal disaster through miscalculation. Third, verbal behavior constitutes an element—by no means all, but an important part—of the complex of signals by which we, to employ Professor Thomas Schelling's definition of deterrence,[2] influence the other side's expectations of our behavior in such a way as to influence its choice of behavior. Not only what we do, but what we say we are doing creates a psychological expectation by the other side that it will not be prevented from acting in accordance with the same principles. Our opponents know that we believe that they believe that they will be acting within the permissible ambit of the principles we ourselves devised. Deterrence cannot be credible if we are ourselves proclaiming the right to do the very thing we wish another superpower to believe we will use force to prevent it from doing. And if deterrence is not credible, it is worse than nothing—a bluff that the other side will call. In this sense, verbal behavior is strategically important in that it can favorably or adversely affect our options in subsequent crises.

The concept of verbal strategy differs from other approaches to verbal behavior in that it proposes the planned, deliberate development and use of principles, concepts, and enunciated norms as a conscious part of the conduct of foreign policy. This does not imply the retrospective use of fanciful apologia for acts already decided upon, nor does it suggest propaganda. Rather, verbal strategy, like other aspects of foreign-policy decision making, introduces into the weighing of policy options an awareness that actions taken must also be explained and that the explanation may be in the long run more costly or more beneficial to the national interest than the act itself. No action should

2. See Thomas C. Schelling, *The Strategy of Conflict,* Cambridge, Mass.: Harvard University Press, 1963, p. 13, hereafter referred to as *The Strategy of Conflict.*

ever be undertaken without assessing the long-run strategic and systemic costs and benefits of what is said to explain and justify the action. Verbal strategy, in other words, requires the same careful planning as any other aspect of strategy for the achievement of national goals. Before an option is chosen, before a verbal strategy is decided upon, its short-, medium-, and long-term effects should be estimated. Such prediction, in turn, involves an effort to predetermine the effect of one's proposed verbal strategy on all the other players in the game, and particularly on one's principal opponent.

Unfortunately, the United States has never learned to listen to itself as if it were the enemy speaking. This study will examine three instances of U.S. verbal behavior in crises of hemispheric solidarity: Guatemala, Cuba, and the Dominican Republic, to show how the explanations of our conduct anticipated the Brezhnev Doctrine. Of course, the recent tragic events in Czechoslovakia are not the same as any of the other events with which they are compared in this study. The United States is not the Soviet Union, and the way the United States used force in Guatemala, Cuba, and the Dominican Republic is different from the way and the circumstances in which the Soviet Union used force against the Czechoslovaks. It is not the purpose of this study to obscure these substantial differences.

If they are obscured, if our behavior in our regional grouping appears very similar to that of the Soviet Union in Eastern Europe, the fault lies at least in part with our verbal strategy. What the U.S. government said in these three instances did not merely serve to describe what was being done, but, bit by bit, laid the basis for a doctrine of world order that encompasses far more than the actions themselves. The cumulative effect of the U.S. pronouncements is to appear to authorize the Soviet Union to do exactly what it did to Czechoslovakia in 1968.

Indeed, the Soviets were able to quote us verbatim to justify their actions. As Hans Morgenthau has said, "What is interesting, and . . . illuminating in these doctrinal arguments is their intellectual similarity. . . ."[3] That this should be so is cause for reexamination of our rhetoric. More than that, it is cause for rethinking the way in which the United States evolves the principles by which it justifies its actions.

The tendency in the pragmatic West is to regard rhetoric at best as ornamentation. What matter what we say, or what the Soviets say? It is what is *done* that counts. Diplomats and statesmen are known after all to be men "paid to lie for their country." Yet the remarkable coincidence of what we *said* in the crises over Guatemala, Cuba, and the Dominican Republic, and what the Soviets *did* in Czechoslovakia, does create the occasion for our looking again at the interaction between word and deed in the contemporary world of nuclear superpowers. This interaction, far from being a matter of purely scholastic interest, occurs at a critical point of congruence between law and strategy, between system building and crisis management.

The analysis of Soviet and American verbal behavior in this study reveals that both we and they have committed ourselves very explicitly to an international system in which two superpowers exercise a kind of eminent domain, each within its geographical region—we in the Americas, or at least in the Central American and Caribbean areas; they in Eastern Europe, with the exception of Yugoslavia. The reaction of most of our press and of political leaders to the Soviet invasion of Czechoslovakia indicates that we are not wholly conscious of, or comfortable with, our agreement to share the world in this way with the Soviets, whatever the advantages in terms of international security. Nor is it clear that we as a people have accepted the limitations such bipolarism imposes on the freedom of others, a freedom this country has in the past championed, and which former Secretary of State Acheson has rightly called "the most revolu-

3.   Hans J. Morgenthau, *A New Foreign Policy for the United States,* New York: Frederick A. Praeger, 1969, p. 113.

tionary and dynamic concept in human history" as well as America's "first line of action" [4] in international strategy. If we have in fact committed ourselves in principle to a world of two superpower "ghettos," then that commitment ought to be the result of a deliberate strategy proceeding from a careful weighing of the short-, medium-, and long-term costs and benefits. It ought not, as we suspect it is, to be the consequence of *post hoc,* inadvertent, strategically deficient verbal conceptualizations emerging as an unintended by-product of the heat of crises.

4.   Dean Acheson's speech to the American Society of Newspaper Editors, April 22, 1950.

2

Czechoslovakia
and the Politics of Invasion

The Czechoslovak invasion has already passed into history and few traces of it as an event remain. Friendship with the Soviet Union was soon resumed by the West. After a brief period of mourning for Czechoslovak freedom, disarmament negotiations, trade, cultural exchanges, and even *détente* were taken up more or less where they had been left off. The event soon became almost a nonevent. Western politicians and students of Russia shrugged and said they had all along expected it, that the Prague liberals had overplayed their hand, that some of us had been foolish and beguiled if we had ever expected Russia to permit the humanization of socialism.

But the invasion did occur; it did catch most observers in both the West and the East by surprise; and it transformed the world as we had learned to see it. Once an event has occurred, it is almost impossible to remember that it had once been virtually unthinkable. This is true of man walking on the moon. It is also true of Russia's return in 1968 to the Stalinist primitivism of the early postwar years. Yet Americans in the spring of 1968 did not believe that the invasion of Czechoslovakia would or could occur, let alone that it would be shrugged off and quickly forgotten.

The Czechoslovaks, by their conduct, made it a costly invasion for the Russians. The horror and brutality visited upon Czechoslovakia showed the world a face of Russia which the cosmetic politics of the Kremlin had worked hard, for a decade, to disguise. Russia's invasion was a policy of desperation arrived at by only the narrowest of Politburo majorities. It was launched after a series of procrastinations. This at least raises the possibility that if the calculable costs of the invasion had been slightly higher, the precarious balance within the Kremlin might have tilted the other way and the invasion might never have taken place.

It is necessary here to recall the momentousness of the events of August 1968, their horror, their poignance, their muddle. Only by remembering events both Russians and Americans would rather forget can we understand that these brutal excesses were not inevitable, that life for small states in a world of superpowers need not necessarily lead every decade to a rape of Prague, that in the 1960's a different normative relationship between superpowers and the smaller states in their region could have evolved in the international system.

There was nothing surprising about the arrival of an unscheduled Aeroflot plane. Aeroflot planes often landed at Prague's Ruzyne Airport on short notice, and when it was announced Tuesday evening, August 20, that a civilian Antonov-24 was due to arrive at ten that night, hardly anyone paid any attention. Nor did it occur to anyone to question why, after the plane had actually landed, it had taxied to the end of the runway only to remain there.

In part, this lack of interest may have been due to the fact that another unscheduled Aeroflot plane, this one from Lvov, arrived only one hour later. This time, however, a number of civilians did disembark. They were greeted with unusual cordiality and respect by customs officials, after which they left the airport, presumably for the center of town. Not that this seemed noteworthy either. Everything soon returned to quiet. Airport officials took a break from their work while waiting for the scheduled flights, one from Bulgaria, another from Yugoslavia, to arrive. The Antonov-24 remained parked at the edge of the runway. Only the customs office seemed brimming with activity. The reason soon became evident.

At 2 A.M., a number of Soviet Aeroflot cars arrived at the airport and quickly discharged a group of civilian and military officials, including a Soviet colonel, all of whom were greeted at the customs office by Colonel Rudolf Stachovsky, chief of passport control at Ruzyne, and Colonel Elias, commander of the Security Air Squadron of the Ministry of Interior. Almost immediately, somehow imperceptibly, the airport seemed to have filled with "suspicious-looking men," men too alert to be tourists or ordinary travelers caught between destinations in the middle of the night.[1] "And then it all began."[2] First, an unannounced

1.   Robert Littell (ed.), *The Czech Black Book* (prepared by the Institute of History of the Czechoslovak Academy of Sciences), New York: Frederick A. Praeger, 1969, pp. 7–9; from an eyewitness account originally published in *Letectvi a Kosmonautica*, August 27, 1968. The dramatic poignance of the destruction of the Prague Spring has been portrayed by a number of writers. For a comprehensive treatment of the Dubcek era and the historical background leading to the Soviet invasion, see Tad Szulc, *Czechoslovakia Since World War II*, New York: The Viking Press, 1971. Szulc was in Prague for a part of the Prague Spring and provides a rare understanding of the dynamics of this experiment. Ivan Sviták, a former Fellow of the Institute of Philosophy of the Czechoslovak Academy of Science, has published an interesting collection of supplementary material which he wrote during the Prague Spring as a leading member of the group of intellectuals associated with *Literarni Listy* that was calling for greater political reform, *The Czechoslovak Experiment 1968–1969*, New York: Columbia University Press, 1971; also see Z. A. B. Zeman, *Prague Spring*, New York: Hill & Wang, 1969; Michael Salomon, *Prague Notebook: The Strangled Revolution*, New York: Little, Brown & Co., 1971.

2.   *Ibid.*

Antonov-12 landed. A contingent of Soviet paratroopers jumped out of the plane and ran toward the tower and the main building. Before they were able to force all persons including airport employees and tourists from the buildings—something which they attempted to do immediately—they were joined on the ground by still more of their kind. The sky now seemed to be raining Soviet aircraft. The Antonov-12's were landing at Ruzyne "in precise one minute intervals," each one disgorging an armed detachment of the Soviet Army.

Gradually, people came to realize why that first plane had remained parked at the end of the runway. The Russians had sent it to replace the control tower; throughout the occupation, it and it alone directed all air traffic in and out of Ruzyne.

By dawn the airport was completely in the hands of the Soviet Army. One eyewitness observed, "People at the airport were slow to grasp what was happening." [3] But they soon understood, since the Russians made all civilians, tourists and employees alike, walk back to Prague on foot. The Soviets did make one minor error, however, in that they forgot to silence the teletype at Ruzyne. This remained "in operation until almost noon," and thus allowed the Czechoslovak people to learn of the dreaded event that they had believed would not happen, another invasion of their country.

But the communication of events did not have to await transmission by teletype. The news of the invasion came directly to most people. Czechoslovakia is a patchwork of roads, a quilt bordered by Austria and West Germany plus four Warsaw Pact powers. Throughout the fateful night of August 20, seemingly endless columns of tanks, armored cars, and army transport vehicles poured across these four frontiers and deposited units in the cities, towns, and villages through which they passed. By 3 A.M., Cierna nad Tisou, nearest the Soviet border, had been occupied; at 3:30, Bratislava, nearest Hungary; by 4, Karlovy Vary, nearest East Germany. Each of these towns recently had been the site

3. *Ibid.*

of a summit conference in which the heads of Czechoslovakia's political system and their counterparts in the Soviet Union and the other Warsaw Pact states had attempted to arrive at a settlement. Before dawn, these cities and every regional capital, Plzen, Ceske Budejovice, Bratislava, Banska Bystrica, Kosice, Ostrava, Hradec, Usti nad Labem, stared into the guns of an occupation —as did Prague.

It has been said that First Secretary Alexander Dubcek and those in his immediate circle had anticipated the invasion beforehand and had set up the underground network within Czechoslovakia that acquitted itself so bravely during the first days of the invasion. This is not entirely true. The resilience of the resistance that greeted the occupation should not belie the fact that it was a spontaneous reaction to a situation that most in Czechoslovakia had considered quite impossible. The Praesidium of the Czechoslovak Central Committee was meeting at the instant the invasion began, for example, to draft a resolution to be submitted before the Extraordinary Fourteenth Party Congress scheduled for September 9. At this meeting, the shock of an entire nation manifested itself in microcosm.

The meeting was being held in the board room of the Praesidium and the entire membership was present. Around midnight, Premier Oldrich Cernik stepped out of the meeting and into the antechamber to receive a call. When he returned, he signaled Dubcek that he wished to speak. The First Secretary interrupted the debate. Cernik declared, "The armies of the five parties have crossed the borders of our Republic and have begun occupying our country." [4] Dubcek's anguish and surprise were immediate. "This is a tragedy, I didn't expect this to happen." [5] An eyewitness observed that Dubcek was not alone in his feelings: "The Presidium was in a state of shock—at least some of

---

4. *Ibid.,* pp. 12–18; from an eyewitness account originally published in *Rude Pravo,* August 23, 1968. For a complementary description of this fateful meeting, see Szulc, *op. cit.,* pp. 372–73.
5. *Ibid.*

its members were. . . ." [6] Dubcek pulled from his files a letter addressed to him on August 19 from the Central Committee of the Communist Party of the Soviet Union and signed by Brezhnev. Dubcek had not read this letter to the Praesidium before, but did so now. Occasionally he stopped to comment. The letter, repeating the allegations of the so-called Warsaw Letter of July 17, 1968, only in more abrupt terms, charged that counterrevolutionary tendencies were running rampant in Czechoslovakia. It now also stated that Dubcek had violated the agreements reached at Cierna and embodied in the Bratislava communiqué. "This is what they keep on saying," Dubcek said, "but they do not take into consideration what the real situation is. After all, we are taking measures." [7] As he approached the end of the letter, which pointedly contained no hint of the invasion, Dubcek interrupted himself to say, "I declare on my honor as a Communist that I had no suspicion, no indication, that anyone would want to undertake such measures against us." Some discussion ensued. The word "tragic" could sometimes be heard in the appalled hush. Dubcek shook his head in disbelief. "That they should have done this to me, after I have dedicated my whole life to cooperation with the Soviet Union, is the great tragedy of my life." [8] Finally, the First Secretary reconvened the Praesidium and announced that they would formulate a proclamation to the nation. They worked until 1:45 A.M. and dispersed at 2 just as the first Soviet planes were beginning to land at Ruzyne. National Assembly Chairman Josef Smrkovsky and Frantisek Kriegel remained by Dubcek's side. They were arrested together.

Only one sentence of the Praesidium's proclamation at first reached the people. "Yesterday, August 20, 1968, around 11 P.M. troops crossed . . ." and then silence. Karel Hoffman, director of the Central Communications Administration, a member of the

6. *Ibid.*
7. *Ibid.*
8. *Ibid.* In his portrayal of Dubcek, Szulc comments, "The first objective fact is that he was—and remains a year after his subsequent fall from power—a loyal and dedicated Communist."

Bilak-Kolder-Indra faction that supported the Soviet position against reform, had ordered dispatchers not to broadcast it and had the medium-wave transmitter shut off. The fact that a man of Hoffman's known sympathies was allowed to remain in control of as crucial an organ as the State Radio, further demonstrates how little the Czechoslovak government had felt in need of precaution and how unexpected the invasion was when it did occur. Gradually, all Czechoslovak radio stations went silent. Immediately, *Vltava,* the voice of the occupation, began to broadcast reports from the Soviet news agency Tass in Czech and Slovak. "Personalities of the Czechoslovak Communist Party," it declared, "requested military aid from the Soviet Union, because our Republic was threatened by counterrevolution. . . ." [9] *Mlada Fronta,* an underground newspaper that went into operation soon after the invasion, commented, "The grammatical errors, the poor pronunciation, the entire style are reminiscent of times one does not forget." [10]

The battle of the radio airwaves had only just begun, however. At 4:30 A.M., Free Radio Prague, despite Hoffman's efforts, succeeded in transmitting the proclamation of the Praesidium to the nation. "The Presidium calls upon all citizens of the Republic to keep the peace and not resist the advancing armies, because the defense of our state borders is now impossible." [11] At 6:35 A.M., the radio appealed to the people to remain calm and to "meet the occupation with passive resistance." At 7:15, citizens were requested not to construct barricades or assemble in large crowds. "Self-control is our best weapon," the radio declared, and later, "We need the streets free." At 7:18, Dubcek's last official pronouncement to the nation prior to his arrest was read: "I beg you to maintain calm and to bear with dignity the present situation." At 7:30, a column of Soviet tanks surrounded the Radio Prague building; at 7:35, they began to fire at it. By 9, the

9. *Ibid.,* p. 19.
10. *Ibid.*
11. *Ibid.,* pp. 10–11.

building was completely destroyed. As it went down, machine-gun and automatic-weapons fire could be heard over the radio—along with the Czechoslovak national anthem.

The Warsaw Pact forces invaded Czechoslovakia prepared for all eventualities except those that greeted them. Every vehicle of the expeditionary force, for example, was painted beforehand with a broad white stripe so that it might be distinguished from those of the Czechoslovak Army should there be resistance, even though this must have been considered extremely unlikely. But the Soviets committed so many blunders during those first days of the invasion that one writer has concluded "no framework for decision had been created." [12]

The Soviets invaded on the evening of August 20 in the knowledge that Deputy Alois Indra was putting before the Praesidium a draft resolution urging the suppression of "reactionary tendencies" in Czechoslovakia. Soviet intelligence indicated that Dubcek would be defeated and that the Praesidium would accept this draft. For this reason the Soviets did not provide in advance for a substitute government. On these same assumptions, no member of the Soviet Politburo journeyed to Prague to direct developments. This left Soviet political interests in the hands of the maladroit Ambassador Chervonenko. It was Chervonenko who had predicted that once Soviet troops arrived, they would be welcomed by major segments of the population.

If the Russians and their Warsaw Pact partners did anything for Czechoslovakia, however, it was to unify the nation. As Frantisek Sorm, chairman of the Czechoslovak Academy of Sciences, wrote to Mstislav Keldysh, president of the Academy of Sciences of the Soviet Union, "the military occupation has

12. Philip Windsor and Adam Roberts, *Czechoslovakia 1968: Reform, Repression and Resistance* (for the Institute for Strategic Studies, London), New York: Columbia University Press, 1969, p. 65; Windsor and Roberts have each written an essay in this collection. The references here are entirely to the essay written by Windsor and entitled "Czechoslovakia, Eastern Europe and Détente."

unified all our people, regardless of their political opinions, into a monolithic whole. . . ." [13]

Not only did the invasion unify a people traditionally divided, it also dissipated their historic pro-Soviet sympathies. *The Czech Black Book* abounds with examples: An official of the Union of Czechoslovak-Soviet Friendship said to Soviet troops, "I have been a Communist and a friend of the Soviet Union for twenty-five years. Ninety per cent of the people stand behind Dubcek. Dubcek wants socialism. Why, then, did you come? " [14] Another citizen wondered, "Why this nervousness? Why this violence? Why the resort to arms? Where is the famous Soviet diplomatic calm and decisiveness? I used to like the Soviet people, especially young people. But looking at the Soviet troops, I was ashamed for my former friendship. Not just for myself, but for them as well." [15] A letter addressed to the Soviet Embassy in Prague read, "The illegal occupation of our country by Warsaw Pact troops is for us, who have always had warm sympathies for the Soviet Union, a deep moral disappointment." [16] Jan Drda wrote in *Rude Pravo,* August 27, "The pen is shaking in my hand, my voice falters. For twenty-five years I have been teaching my children to love the Soviet Union. . . . All this is in ruins now." [17] A special edition of *Student,* addressing itself on August 24 to Leonid Brezhnev, declared, "It may not matter to you, but somewhere in Europe there are several million people who hate you! " [18]

In assuming that there would be those who would emerge to form a collaborationist regime, in believing that their forces would be welcomed by pro-Soviet elements within the population, the Soviets clearly miscalculated. This fact was not lost on the

13. *The Czech Black Book,* p. 164.
14. *Ibid.,* p. 34.
15. *Ibid.,* p. 37.
16. *Ibid.,* p. 119.
17. *Ibid.,* pp. 237–38.
18. *Ibid.,* pp. 156–57.

Czechoslovaks themselves. On August 27, *Politika* remarked, "It seems that the espionage network in this country flopped, and the standard of the work of the Soviet diplomats in Prague is indicated by its results." [19]

Two contributing factors held the people together and allowed them to function with single-minded cohesion. The first, perhaps the foremost, was that a free government continued to exist. The Extraordinary Fourteenth Congress of the Communist Party was held not on September 9 but on August 22, the day after the invasion. Delegates from all over Czechoslovakia— 1,192 of the 1,543 scheduled to attend—journeyed to a factory in Prague-Vysocany. "It was a truly historic congress . . ." *Svoboda* reported on August 24. "Every delegate present had carried, as the saying goes, his skin to the market." [20] Throughout the first week of the occupation, the congress publicly sanctioned the resistance and saw to it that democratic processes continued. A petition circulated among the people of Gottwaldov received over twenty thousand signatures recalling pro-Soviet Deputy Alois Indra from his post as representative from their district. The second unifying factor was the flourishing underground press. *Rude Pravo* hardly missed an issue and in fact was joined by a myriad of other publications, such as *Politika, Student, Svoboda, Lidova Demokracie,* many of which were no more than sheets of mimeographed paper. Thanks to these publications, the people of Prague were able to organize perfectly coordinated stoppages and strikes.

The resistance went through various phases. First, the underground instructed the people to engage the troops in conversation; then the order went out to ignore them completely. Overnight,

19. *Ibid.,* pp. 231–32. Szulc, *op. cit.,* p. 383, concurs: ". . . the so-called allied troops entered Czechoslovakia expecting a quick military and political triumph, but discovered, literally within minutes, how atrociously the Kremlin planners had misunderstood and misinterpreted the situation in the country. In fact, things went wrong from the very first moment . . ."
20. *Ibid.,* pp. 83–84.

Prague became a city without street signs or addresses. There were many streets that retained a name during the occupation, but that name was Dubcek. The widely publicized fact that Soviet troops actually began to falter as the occupation progressed is proof enough of the pressure the Czechoslovaks were able to muster through discipline and unity. The Soviets, expecting a good portion of the population to assist their troops, had made inadequate provision for the supply of food. This gave the Czechoslovaks added leverage which they used determinedly.

Soviet troops took to senseless shooting during the night. As *Lidova Demokracie* reported August 26, 1968, "The night belongs to the occupiers, to their helpless rage; the day belongs to the people of Prague." [21] The suicide of a Soviet soldier who could not bear the truth the Czechoslovaks brought home to him, reveals the people's power in the midst of their powerlessness. This, too, the Czechoslovaks realized. Demonstrating extraordinary political acumen, *Slova Svobody* wrote:

> The peculiarity and extraordinariness of our present situation rest in the fact that circumstances do not allow any political compromise. If only every Czech would understand that there is no way out, then perhaps our "allies," the occupiers, would see it too. It is not our turn now; and our Warsaw Pact partners are in the unenviable position in which there is no move by which they could win the match. They have only two alternatives—to admit, sportsmanlike, that they have lost, or to kick the chessboard. Kick it with brutality but at the same time with complete impotence, for the greatest power is now the same as the greatest powerlessness.[22]

But Czechoslovak power lasted only as long as Czechoslovak unity. In the end, the people were demoralized, not by Soviet tanks, but by their leader's acceptance of Soviet demands. The August 27 communiqué from Moscow, Kai Hermann reported,

21. *Ibid.,* p. 197.
22. *Ibid.,* pp. 182–83.

came as "almost as grave a shock as the invasion a week earlier." [23] The Czechoslovaks had to swallow what the Russians knew would disillusion them, the bowing of the Dubcek regime to the superior weight of the Soviet Union. As Richard Lowenthal comments: ". . . the Kremlin seems to have calculated that if it had been forced for the moment to deal with the rightful leaders of Czechoslovakia, the latter had been forced to take the first step towards recognising the superior right of occupation, and that time and the weight of Soviet physical presence would gradually push them further along that road. And this time, the Soviets did *not* miscalculate." [24] It was not the same Dubcek who returned to his nation; his compromise led to their disintegration.

The reason was simple: in terms of the occupation, even partial legitimacy was sufficient. This the Czechoslovaks had known. Throughout the resistance, they realized that they had one task: to prevent the Warsaw Powers acquiring any justification for their invasion from what the Czechoslovaks themselves did. "Nothing had been organized," Kai Hermann wrote, "but everybody, somehow, seemed to know what to do." [25] After the initial shock of the invasion, the Czechoslovak underground understood that any direct confrontation would be futile and would lend greater credence to the Soviet contention that reactionary elements were at work. Free Radio Prague was once called upon to deny rumors alleging that Dubcek was dead. "It is probably a provocation aimed at inciting people to react violently against the occupiers . . ." the Radio concluded.[26] The violence occurred mostly the first night, before the word went out to resist passively. After that—to cite one measure taken to prevent provocation of the Soviet troops—liquor sales were restricted. Czechoslovak

23. Kai Hermann, "The Fall of Prague," *Encounter,* 31 (November 1968), pp. 85–93; reference is found on p. 85.
24. Richard Lowenthal, "The Sparrow in the Cage (II)," *Encounter,* 32 (February 1969), pp. 80–90; specific reference is on p. 86.
25. Hermann, *loc. cit.,* p. 86. Szulc also claims that the resistance began spontaneously, *op. cit.,* p. 383.
26. *The Czech Black Book,* p. 138.

youth removed swastikas they had put up in protest against the Soviet Union; they realized that the occupying troops might regard this as evidence that German revanchists were indeed active in Prague. Eventually the Russians had to give up the pretext of direct foreign intervention. It was at this point that they turned to the doctrine of limited sovereignty and socialist solidarity.

We know little of what went into the Soviet decision to invade. It appears to several authorities that China was uppermost in Kremlin considerations. Harrison E. Salisbury reports a young Kremlin official stating: "Our leadership is very concerned about the situation with China. The leaders feel that anything may happen. In such a situation they cannot even consider the possibility of criticism from within the country. They think this might weaken us. It is the same as their reaction to Czechoslovakia. They thought Czechoslovakia would not be reliable if war came in the Far East. China and the Chinese crisis are the root of the problem." [27] The last straw, some Kremlin-watchers speculate, was the success of the West German government in forging new links with the countries of Eastern Europe. This view of their own downfall was particularly shared by the Dubcek men in Prague. Attractive offers, particularly in the form of credits for needed capital improvements, came from West Germany. Such offers had been sought eagerly by the orthodox regimes of East Germany and Poland. Made to the liberal regime in Prague, the offers were seen in Pankow, Warsaw, and Moscow as brazen attempts to lure an unstable satellite out of the Communist camp. Poland, East Germany, and Czechoslovakia formed an "iron triangle," representing the most highly industrialized, economically important region inside the Soviet hegemony outside the Soviet Union. Although the integration of East European industry was far from accomplished, to a limited extent Czechoslovak nuts and Polish bolts had deliberately been made to depend on each other. Soviet intervention in Czechoslovakia thus forestalled any ten-

27. *The New York Times,* May 27, 1969, p. 6.

dency toward cracks in the triangle, particularly at a time of perceived Chinese threats to Russia's other borders.

Other authorities, particularly men like Ota Sik who were intimately involved in the restructuring of Czechoslovak socialism —the "socialism with human face" experiment—tended to see the invasion as part of the resurgence of orthodoxy in Moscow. In their opinion, it was the Russian Communist leaders' fears of the latent and not-so-latent tendencies toward liberalization in their own country, more than the threat from Peking, that most influenced the men of the Kremlin. In favor of this theory it may be noted that all the whiffs of socialist democracy which were so apparent in the spring air of Prague could also be sniffed, if faintly, in the heavier, colder climate of Moscow: the "cosmo-politan" writers, the "negative" poets, the physicists daring to dabble in civil liberties, the "market" economists. Evidently the place to stop this kind of rot was at its source, in Prague.

All these reasons no doubt converged to urge strong Soviet measures. Nevertheless, the most striking characteristic of Soviet behavior in the periods just before and after the invasion is its indecisiveness and unpredictability. "Evidence of division and vacillation in the collective leadership is conclusive," writes Richard Lowenthal, "not only for the week preceding the crucial decision, but even after it. More, the decision may be said to have remained incomplete in important aspects for over a month after the invasion." [28] Anatole Shub, *Washington Post* correspondent in Moscow at the time of the invasion, argues that the world had been led to believe that political agreements at Cierna and Bratislava had resolved the differences between the Czechoslovak and Soviet Politburos. Citing a Yugoslav writer, Shub argues that "Czechoslovakia provided a case, virtually unique in modern history, where enormous military forces were unleashed after the climax in tension had passed, with scarcely any new preparation of world or Soviet domestic opinion for such drastic

28. Lowenthal, "The Sparrow in the Cage (I)," *Encounter,* 32 (January 1969), pp. 87–96; specific reference on p. 87.

action." [29] In the dance of the world's leviathans, sudden, surprising new steps or tempi are introduced only at considerable risk. Such risk may be warranted in order to gain a major strategic advantage. But if Soviet behavior toward Czechoslovakia was intended to catch everyone by surprise, it succeeded only in a bizarre way. After a summer of threats, showdowns, and military maneuvers, the remarkable thing about the invasion was not only that it took place, but also that it was managed so badly, so erratically, with so many fitful starts and stops, and launched at the very time the invaders had pledged themselves to a policy of nonintervention. Shub concludes that it was Soviet hesitations caused by divisions among, and in the minds of, the leaders that prompted them to act so unpredictably. In reference to the meetings at Cierna and Bratislava, Philip Windsor writes, "It was before these meetings that most people in the West suddenly came to the conclusion that Soviet military action was after all a possibility; and that after the meetings it was generally assumed that it was now unlikely. . . . The invasion when it did come, took almost everyone by surprise—not only in the West but also in Czechoslovakia." [30] In this special sense, Russian conduct was highly unpredictable, surprising.

What is relevant here is not the fact of unpredictability alone, but rather the fact that the Russians *felt free* to act unpredictably. The significance of this should not be minimized. As Yugoslav Professor Leo Mates states, "If it is possible for unprovoked military intervention to follow negotiations and agreement, then the danger to peace is transferred to the domain of the unpredictable, which can but leave deep traces on the general behavior of states in international relations." [31] The Soviets took

29. Anatole Shub, "Lessons of Czechoslovakia," *Foreign Affairs,* 47 (January 1969), pp. 266–80; reference on p. 267.

30. Windsor, *op. cit.,* p. 65. Szulc, *op. cit.,* p. 378, comments that "Perhaps the most valuable element in the Soviet stratagem was the West's psychological inability to believe that the Kremlin would actually stage an invasion."

31. Cited in Shub, *loc. cit.,* p. 267.

a precipitous action: they invaded Czechoslovakia when it was least expected and felt that they could do so without provoking the United States. The issue here is not whether the United States should have taken steps to defend Czechoslovakia; rather it is whether the signals emitted by the United States led Soviet policy makers to conclude that they could act as they did with impunity. Implied in Soviet conduct is the assertion that not only could they invade a satellite, but that they could deceive, lie, confuse, and surprise the world; so long as their conduct was confined to their private ghetto of vassal states, they could be as erratic, unsystematic, unpredictable and immoral as they pleased. Implied also is the notion, correct as it turned out, that what Russia did in its own ghetto would make little more difference to the rest of the world, and to the conduct of the United States in particular, than what the Soviet leaders were doing to dissidents within the Soviet Union itself. That the Russians presumed on their relations with the United States government in this manner, speaks not only of them but of the United States, the nature of its rhetoric, its pattern of deterrent signals, and the overall conduct of its foreign relations.

Shub, Windsor, Lowenthal, and others all contend that hesitations and doubts plagued Soviet policy makers throughout this episode. Philip Windsor writes:

> If one assumes, first, that the Soviet leaders were not divided or indecisive and that they were all fully prepared to invade Czechoslovakia, one has to account for the fact that they first made such difficulties about the venue and timing of the meeting that was subsequently held at Cierna (Mr. Dubcek's refusal to go to Moscow would have given them at that moment a much better opportunity to claim that the Warsaw Pact was in danger than subsequently, and at least as good an opportunity as they later had to claim that they were responding to some kind of Czech invitation); second, why they did not act while their troops were in the country after the manoeuvres; third, why they allowed their own situation in the Eastern bloc to deteriorate disastrously in

the meantime by giving Marshal Tito the opportunity to make his spectacularly successful visit to Prague, and allowing the emergence of an embryonic alignment between Czechoslovakia, Yugoslavia and Rumania; fourth, why it was deemed advisable for Herr Ulbricht to visit Czechoslovakia during the same period if it was not in the hope of continuing the diplomacy that had followed from the Warsaw letter and the Dresden meeting; finally, why they gave the other Communist parties time to prepare their own interventions on behalf of Czechoslovakia, express confidence in the Soviet Union in the period thereafter, and then round on it all the more fiercely when they found their confidence had been misplaced.[32]

Richard Lowenthal suggests that the decision in principle to invade Czechoslovakia was probably taken at the end of June after the publication of the "Two Thousand Words." [33] What is striking about the behavior of the Soviet Politburo in the period following, however, is that it did waver. Soviet troops on maneuvers entered Czechoslovakia on June 20 and remained long after July 2, when they were due to leave. General Prchlik's refusal to accept the legality of their prolonged presence caused Dubcek to relieve him of his duties. Windsor even suggests that this "exercise" should be seen as the first of what were really two Soviet military interventions. Why, Windsor asks, did the Russians then withdraw their troops in July, giving the Czechoslovak leadership time to strengthen its diplomatic position? The answer is that behind the hesitation and vacillation of the Soviet Union's "collective leadership" was a deeply divided Soviet Politburo. These divisions within the Kremlin reflected an awareness of the poten-

32. *Ibid.,* p. 66.
33. Lowenthal, *Encounter* (February 1969), p. 80. On June 27, 1968, a manifesto entitled "Two Thousand Words" was published by three major Prague newspapers and by a weekly literary journal, *Literarni Listy.* The document, written by the novelist Ludvik Vaculik, endorsed by a group of seventy leading intellectuals and other public figures, called for a purge of conservatives from government and opposed external, that is, Soviet, intervention in Czechoslovak affairs. Szulc, *op. cit.,* pp. 341–46 reproduces it in its entirety.

tial cost of an invasion in terms of world opinion, Russia's relationship to the Third World, the carefully cultivated resumption of friendship with Tito, and the links with nonruling Communist parties throughout the world. All of these Soviet interests were bound, to some extent, to suffer from any military move to crush Czechoslovakia. The differences within the Kremlin appear to have turned on the order of magnitude of these costs and on their relative importance as against the threat of liberalization in Eastern Europe.

White House adviser on Soviet Affairs Helmut Sonnenfeldt has warned against classifying the members of the Soviet Politburo into "doves" and "hawks." [34] This is good advice. Reifications do not help to explain the division of opinion in the Soviet Politburo over the decision to invade Czechoslovakia. Without imposing any false structure of rationality on the men in the Kremlin, it is safe to assume that systematic calculations of the risks involved, costs anticipated, and benefits to be derived had more to do with their deliberations than did their personality traits, particularly those which could be described by the expressions "dove" and "hawk." It is reasonable to assume that all Soviet leaders are approximately equally tough and approximately equally flexible. In the case of Czechoslovakia, it was probably their different perceptions of the costs that led them to different positions. Robert Littell suggests that "according to excellent sources in Moscow," the eventual lineup in the "sharply divided" Politburo was 7 to 4 in favor of the invasion, with Suslov, Kosygin, Podgorny, and Voronov opposed.[35]

What appears to have prompted Suslov to oppose the invasion was "his belief in the magic power of ideological formulations to mould the policy of communist parties anywhere," [36] and

---

34. In a statement before the New York University Center for International Studies Conference on the International Effects of the Invasion of Czechoslovakia held in New York, December 6, 1968.
35. Editor's Introduction, *The Czech Black Book*, pp. v–x.
36. Lowenthal, *Encounter* (February 1969), p. 83.

his fear that the invasion would scrap the world conference of communist parties "on which he had worked so long even before it started." [37] Philip Windsor concurs: "Mr. Suslov, the Party's chief ideologue, who has long had a reputation as an extremely tough man, is reported to have been most reluctant to invade. 'If we go in,' he is quoted as saying, 'we might as well abandon the conference here and now.' " [38] Suslov was conspicuously absent from the high-level meeting in Warsaw in July which drafted the Warsaw Letter, and did not speak at the meeting of the Central Committee held on July 17 to approve it. "Though the approval was now described as 'unanimous,' " writes Lowenthal, "the original decision of the Politburo clearly was not. . . ." [39] Lowenthal argues that the inclusion in the Soviet delegation to Warsaw of Pyotr Shelest, who opposed the liberalizing developments in Czechoslovakia, "was as revealing as the absence of Suslov. . . ." [40] The fact that Suslov and Boris N. Ponomarev, in charge of relations with the world's nonruling Communist parties, did not speak at the plenary meeting of the Central Committee of the Soviet Union on July 17, while men "in the control of Soviet intellectuals," such as M. V. Keldysh and N. M. Gribachev, did, reveals that the policies reflected in the Warsaw Letter and the events that followed were a victory of those favoring Soviet internal and regional interests over those concentrating on ideological principles or international ambitions.

Kosygin and Podgorny may well have refused to accept the policy expressed in the Warsaw Letter on these grounds. To do so, both men probably realized, would set back one of Russia's prime foreign-policy objectives, the disintegration of NATO. In the two years preceding the invasion, Soviet policy makers had been attempting to exploit the attitudes generated in Europe by the *détente* in order to bring about the dissolution of NATO. In

37. Peter Grose in *The New York Times,* May 29, 1969, p. 4.
38. Windsor, *op. cit.,* p. 73.
39. Lowenthal, *Encounter* (February 1969), p. 81.
40. *Ibid.*

the summer of 1966, at the end of a conference in Bucharest, the Warsaw Pact partners had announced that they favored the development of a "European security system" involving, first, recognition of the territorial *status quo* in Europe and, second, the dissolution of both the Warsaw Pact and NATO in favor of a new all-European defense system. As Lowenthal points out, the Bucharest declaration, which embodied these proposals, said nothing of the bilateral treaty arrangements between the Soviet Union and the nations of Eastern Europe. These agreements would have allowed Soviet troops to remain "on the Elbe even after the dissolution of the Warsaw Pact, while the Americans would have had to go home after the dissolution of NATO." [41]

Russia thus had invested some effort in a campaign to loosen the bloc system in Europe, a campaign that an invasion of Czechoslovakia was bound to defeat. There were members of the Politburo, Kosygin in particular, who had led this campaign and continued to give it priority. Windsor suggests that the emergency meeting of the Central Committee on August 19 may have been called to allow the plenary to act as a referee in the dispute of the Politburo. Lowenthal further indicates that it may well have been their distrust of each other that prompted the members of the Politburo, with the exception of two who remained in Moscow to manage subsidiary affairs, to leave Russian territory and travel to Cierna nad Tisou. In October 1956, during even the worst moments of that crisis, no more than four officials in the Praesidium went to Poland and no more than two went to Hungary at the same time. In regard to the Cierna conference, however, "the members of the collective [the Politburo] knew that some of them would apply more exacting standards of compliance than others, and they evidently could not agree on trusting a single leader, or even a 'troika,' with deciding in their name." [42] For this reason it was the Soviets and not the Czecho-

41. Lowenthal, *Encounter* (January 1969), p. 90.
42. Lowenthal, *Encounter* (February 1969), p. 82. For an excellent description of the Cierna meeting, see Szulc, *op. cit.,* pp. 361–65,

slovaks who wavered at Cierna. The Czechoslovaks stood up to the Russians and were not divided. Dubcek reportedly rejected an attempt by Brezhnev to specify the names of "reactionaries" in Czechoslovakia on the grounds that this represented an unacceptable interference in his country's internal affairs. The Soviets had counted on being able to induce the conservative elements in the Czechoslovak elite to take a more affirmative stand against Dubcek or, at least, to be able to break up his liberal support into factions. They in no way succeeded. For this reason they returned to Moscow with only general assurances from Dubcek and the Czechoslovak Praesidium rather than specific commitments.

The crisis of confidence within the Soviet Politburo seems to have continued even in the days immediately after the invasion, as Windsor points out. Announcement of all major decisions are customarily made over the signatures of the ruling triumvirate of Brezhnev, Kosygin, and Podgorny. This is intended to underscore the importance of a particular matter, but, more, to demonstrate the unanimity of the government and Party in regard to a specific decision. These signatures were conspicuously absent during the first five days of the invasion. That an invasion had occurred was initially announced in the name of Tass. *Pravda* published a defense of the action on the second day but this too went unsigned. The first official document concerning the invasion was published on the fourth day in the name of the five occupying partners. Windsor underlines the importance of this. "Throughout these days," he comments, "there was no official statement, either on behalf of the government of the Soviet Union or that of the CPSU, about the invasion; not one of the three men signed anything; and the governmental statements, as distinct from the polemics of *Pravda,* were confined to the committee rooms of the Kremlin." [43] It would seem that the dynamics that prompted the entire Politburo to travel en masse to Cierna remained the same even after Soviet troops had moved.

43. Windsor, *op. cit.,* p. 67.

The costs and benefits as perceived by the members of the Politburo were nicely balanced. Given that balance, it can be argued that the decision to invade could have gone the other way. The Soviets might have been deterred from acting against Czechoslovakia through direct invasion had there been an added cost, namely, a convincing uncertainty about the risk of a U.S. military reaction. Had they felt that too great a risk existed, had they felt more uncertain about what the United States might do, they might have acted in a more restrained manner toward Czechoslovakia. There was, however, no cause for such uncertainty. The Russians were able to point out that in Czechoslovakia they were merely applying the very principles of conduct the United States had evolved in relation to Latin America. As we shall see, our prior verbal strategy in asserting U.S. rights over Latin America provided the Soviet leaders with clear, even if unintended guidelines. By staying well within the guidelines the United States itself had devised, the Soviets were able to reduce the risk of a U.S. military reaction.

We also know that Soviet leaders contemplating the invasion of a "sovereign fraternal state" were concerned about another possible cost: the effect on Communist and Soviet world prestige. To some members of the Politburo this consideration made the entire operation untenable, whatever the benefits of enforced conformity and loyalty. To others, the price was right for the perceived gains. But what if the cost had been even higher, as it would have been if the United States by its own conduct and principles had not already helped endorse a two-ghetto approach to the international system? Might the price then not have been too high for one or several of those, even, who supported the invasion?

The Kremlin leaders were spared this more difficult decision. The American pot had already disqualified itself from calling the Soviet kettle black.

3

The Brezhnev Doctrine

THE BREZHNEV PRINCIPLES

On September 25, 1968, *Pravda* published an article titled "Sovereignty and International Duties of Socialist Countries." [1] Defending the invasion by the Warsaw Pact nations, this document argues that Czechoslovakia "is responsible not only to its own people, but also to all the socialist countries. . . ." It reasons that as a "socialist state, staying in a system of other states composing the socialist community," Czechoslovakia cannot exercise its sovereignty in a way "opposed to the interests of the world of socialism" because the "weakening of any of the links in the world system of socialism directly affects all the socialist countries, which cannot look indifferently upon this."

The *Pravda* article further contends that "when a danger arises to socialism itself in a particular country," when a socialist state permits "encroachment on the foundations of socialism, on the basic principles of Marxism-Leninism," when "anti-socialist and revisionist elements . . . under the guise of 'democratization' . . . befog the minds of the masses, stealthily hatching a

---

1. Reprinted in the translation of the Soviet press agency, *The New York Times*, September 27, 1968, p. 3.

counter-revolutionary coup," and they are "not duly rebuffed in-side the country" then the socialist community may act jointly to protect the sovereignty of that member of the community threatened by the force of "world imperialism" supported by in-ternal subversive "anti-socialist forces." Such an action on the part of the socialist community is not illegal, *Pravda* argues, be-cause the ordinary yardstick of international law does not apply within the community. "Those who speak about the 'illegal ac-tions' of the allied socialist countries in Czechoslovakia forget that in a class society there is not and there cannot be non-class laws. Laws and legal norms are subjected to the laws of the class struggle, the laws of social development."

In other words, according to these concepts, any socialist country's sovereignty is invariably subject to the norms of the socialist community. Therefore, no socialist state should expect to rely on such international legal concepts as self-determination, coexistence, or the right not to be coerced by other states. Apply-ing these principles in the specific instance led their proponents to conclude that when Czechoslovakia was found by the other members of the socialist community to be in danger of drifting into alien heresy, then the community had the right to use force to save Czechoslovak socialism and the community's solidarity.

This is the essence of the doctrine enunciated by *Pravda* and known as the Brezhnev Doctrine. It was elaborated by Soviet Foreign Minister Gromyko at the U.N. General Assembly:

> The countries of the socialist commonwealth have their own vital interests, their own obligations, including those of safeguarding their mutual security and their own socialist principles of mutual relations based on fraternal assistance, solidarity and internationalism. This common-wealth constitutes an inseparable entity cemented by un-breakable ties such as history has never known. . . . The Soviet Union and other socialist countries have on many occasions warned those who are tempted to try to roll back

the socialist commonwealth, to snatch at least one link from
it, that we will neither tolerate nor allow that to happen.[2]

And what of national freedom and self-determination? "It seems
to be difficult for [representatives of the imperialist camp] to
realize," Gromyko pronounced, "that socialism really and genuinely does settle the national question."

Once a state becomes a member of the Soviet bloc, it must
remain one for all time. Mr. Gromyko indicated that the "Soviet
Union deems it necessary to proclaim from this rostrum, too,
that the socialist states cannot and will not allow a situation
where the vital interests of socialism are infringed upon and
encroachments are made on the inviolability of the boundaries
of the socialist commonwealth and, therefore, on the foundations of international peace."

Other Soviet writers have had their turn at sweeping up the
embarrassing debris left by the invasion. "The lessons of history," according to the *New Times* of Moscow, "show that only
in the mighty socialist community is the freedom and independence of Czechoslovakia's peoples reliably guaranteed."[3] From
this assumption it follows that anything conducing to "socialist
solidarity" *ipso facto* advances Czechoslovak freedom. This
freedom is to be found in strict adherence to orthodox socialism
as defined by the other states of the community. Any attempt by
a people to achieve any other kind of freedom outside the norms
of socialist solidarity is myopic and constitutes aggression against
both self and community. True, First Secretary Dubcek and
the other Czechoslovak leaders pleaded that far from yielding
to capitalism, they were strengthening communism by making it
more acceptable to their people, that the Party was "trying to
show that it is capable of a different political leadership and

2. A. Gromyko, addressing the U.N. General Assembly, U.N. Doc.
   A/PV.1679, 3 October 1968, p. 26 at pp. 30–31.
3. *New Times* (a weekly journal of world affairs, published by Trud,
   Moscow), 43, October 30, 1968, p. 15.

management than the discredited bureaucratic-police methods, mainly by the strength of its Marxist-Leninist ideas, by the strength of its programme, its just policy supported by all the people." [4] But one man's liberalization is another's subversion. The leaders of the five Warsaw Pact nations were deeply concerned by the permissiveness of the Dubcek regime towards emergent non-Communist elements in Czechoslovak public life. "The forces of reaction," these leaders said, were "taking advantage of the weakening of the party leadership of the country" in order "to undermine the socialist system, to set Czechoslovakia against the other socialist countries." [5] In the spring and summer of 1968, as *New Times* viewed it from Moscow, "Czechoslovakia became a focal point in the struggle between the forces of imperialist reaction and counter-revolution, on the one hand, and the forces of socialism, on the other. A deadly threat arose to the socialist state. The anti-socialist forces sought to divert the Czechoslovak people from their socialist path, to restore a bourgeois order in that country and sever it from the socialist community. Things reached a point when five socialist states saw no alternative but to send troops to the assistance of the Czechoslovak people." [6] As seen from Moscow or Pankow, it was the failure of the Prague leaders to perceive the danger to their own people that made it necessary for others with better perspective to come to the rescue of socialist legality and socialist order.

The rescuing Warsaw Pact troops claimed to have arrived in the nick of time to preserve freedom and democracy. "The anti-socialist forces in Czechoslovakia, which worked systematically for months to undermine the prestige of the Communist

4. Reply of the Praesidium of the Czechoslovak Communist Party Central Committee to the Warsaw Letter of July 18, 1968, in *The Times* of London, July 19, 1968, p. 8.
5. Five Power Letter, or "the Warsaw Letter," criticizing events in Czechoslovakia, published July 17, 1968, in *The Times* of London, July 19, 1968, p. 8.
6. *New Times*, 35, September 4, 1968, p. 1.

Party and to deprive it of its leading role, created a situation which could have led to the restoration of capitalism in Czechoslovakia and a reorientation of her foreign policy." [7] To protect "the principles of proletarian internationalism, the Soviet Union and the other socialist countries have undertaken joint actions for the defense of the achievements of socialism in fraternal Czechoslovakia . . . against the encroachments of domestic and foreign enemies . . . and toward insuring the conditions for the free development of a sovereign socialist country. . . ." [8] It was not that the Czechoslovak leaders were a part of this conspiracy. Rather, the problem was that they did not recognize the power and the subtlety of the forces of counterrevolution which were threatening to displace them and to transform de-Stalinization into de-socialization.

In other words, it is for the socialist community and not just for the government of Czechoslovakia, to determine when Czechoslovak freedom, which is to say its socialist orthodoxy, is endangered, and, accordingly, to determine when to react with force. The community demands "sincere co-operation on the basis of mutual respect, equality, territorial integrity, independence and socialist solidarity," [9] but with a new emphasis on the last two words. When elements within a member state threaten socialist solidarity, the community must take preventive military action. A state invaded in such circumstances has no cause to complain, for such a preventive intervention by its allies "fully accords with the right of states to individual or collective self-defence envisaged in the treaties of alliance concluded between the fraternal socialist countries." [10] Above all, the law of the socialist community decrees firmly and finally that "no one will ever be allowed to wrest a single component of the

7. *Ibid.*, p. 2.
8. *Kommunist,* April 21, 1969.
9. *New Times,* 35, September 4, 1968, p. 1.
10. Tass Statement of the Events in Czechoslovakia, *Documents,* supplement to *New Times,* 35, September 4, 1968, p. 30.

38   *Word Politics*

community of socialist states from it" [11]—not even the misguided leaders of a deviating state itself.

To allay lingering doubts about the morality and legality of their conduct, the Warsaw Pact nations averred, at least initially, that their military entry into Czechoslovakia was in "response to the call for help addressed to us by Czechoslovak Party and government leaders loyal to the cause of socialism:" [12] not necessarily the constitutionally authorized leaders, but those most loyal to the norms of the community and most aware of the danger to its solidarity. Although Czechoslovak Foreign Minister Hajek told the Security Council on August 24, 1968, that the invasion "did not take place upon request or demand of the Czechoslovak Government nor of any other constitutional organs of this Republic" [13] any call, however faint, by an orthodox faction, however weak, suffices, according to the principles of the new doctrine, to validate massive military intervention.

Such action of collective self-defense, a rescue operation by the community, is purely a family matter and none of the neighbors' business. When certain members of the United Nations sought to take up the matter in the Security Council, they were bluntly rebuffed by Mr. Malik, the Soviet Union's representative:

> The events taking place in Czechoslovakia are a matter for the Czechoslovak people and the States of the socialist community, linked together as they are by common responsibilities, and are a matter for them alone. . . . None of them has asked for a meeting of the Security Council, not only because they regard it as unnecessary in the present circumstances but also because they consider the matter as lying outside the purview of the Security Council.[14]

11. *Ibid.*
12. Appeal to the Citizens of the Czechoslovak Socialist Republic by the Warsaw Pact governments, *ibid.*, p. 30.
13. J. Hajek, addressing the Security Council, U.N. Doc. S/PV.1445, 24 August 1968, p. 96.
14. J. Malik, addressing the Security Council, U.N. Doc. S/PV.1441, 21 August 1968, pp. 48–50.

The Czechoslovaks, left thus to struggle alone within the Socialist encampment, understood the futility of armed resistance and in time were forced to give at least lip service to "proletarian internationalism"—the Brezhnev Doctrine.[15]

In summary, the Soviet view of recent events in Czechoslovakia gives rise to a number of normative propositions:

1. A nation-member of a regional or ideological community cannot ever be withdrawn or withdraw itself from that community's jurisdiction.

2. The community may impose standards of behavior on its members in the realm of domestic and foreign policy. These are designed to ensure that the community and its prevailing sociopolitical system will survive and that the security of its members is protected against the Enemy within and without. Adherence to these minimum rules or standards constitutes an obligatory duty of membership in the community.

3. Whether a member of the community is living up to these normative obligations in any given instance is determined by the other members of the community, and not by the unilateral self-determination of any single member.

4. If the other members determine that one member is in dereliction of its duties, they may use various degrees of force, including military, to alter the policies and government of the delinquent. Such use of force is not aggression but rather the opposite: collective self-defense, an action in which the community organization is defending itself, its sacrosanct collective integrity, against the encroachment of an alien ideology.

5. In particular, any socioeconomic or political doctrine or system which varies from the one exclusively established in the community is by definition alien, and its espousal, even by the citizens and government of a member of the community, in effect constitutes foreign subversion of, and aggression against,

15. Cf., e.g., *The New York Times,* October 19, 1968, p. 2.

the community in response to which collective force may be used in self-defense.

6. The territory of a member-state of the community may be invaded by the armies of the other states acting collectively under the treaty of the community in response to a summons by any persons the community designates as loyalist "leaders" of the invaded state, even though these are not recognized as the legal government of that state even by the other members of the community.

U.S. REPUDIATION OF THE BREZHNEV PRINCIPLES

The news of the Warsaw Pact nations' invasion of Czechoslovakia, as Secretary of State Rusk said, "sent a shock wave of indignation and apprehension around the world. . . ." [16] The United States reacted with proper indignation at this blatant violation of human dignity and international law. "The cynicism of the Kremlin move, made in violation of the most elementary canons of international law," *The New York Times* declared on the morning of the invasion, "is underlined by the bare-faced hypocrisy of the Tass claim that the invasion was made at the request of Czechoslovak Government and Communist Party leaders." [17] President Johnson spoke for all humanity when he said, "The tragic news from Czechoslovakia shocks the conscience of the world." [18] Richard Nixon, then campaigning for the Presidency, described the Soviet action as "an outrage against the conscience of the world. . . ."

Secretary of State Dean Rusk outlined the position of the

16. D. Rusk, addressing the General Assembly, Press Release USUN–155 (68), October 2, 1968.
17. *The New York Times,* August 21, 1968, editorial page.
18. Soviet Intervention in Czechoslovakia: Statement by President Johnson, United States, Department of State, *Bulletin,* LIX, September 1968, p. 261.

United States in greater detail. United States interest in the situation in Czechoslovakia was based on our concern that "a small country . . . live its own life. . . ." Russia's excuses were "patently contrived," Rusk declared.[19] Reacting to the principles of the Brezhnev Doctrine, the United States at once took the position that it sought to establish new rules of international conquest. We asserted that these proposed rules violated existing international law and custom, that they introduced a dangerous new element of unpredictability and instability into world politics, and, finally, that they sought to create an authoritarian, bipolar system repugnant to our basic concepts of national sovereignty and freedom.

In the United Nations, the U.S. delegate to the U.N. Special Committee on Principles of International Law, Herbert Reis, stressed that Soviet behavior in Czechoslovakia stood in baleful contrast to Russia's own high-minded rhetoric at the United Nations and elsewhere. Reis quoted Gromyko as having said as recently as September 22, 1967, that "peaceful coexistence would become a farce" if it were not "applied in even measure to all states, large and small, and to all regions of the world." Reis reminded the Soviet Union of its promise, in the era of the de-Stalinizing Twentieth Party Congress, to accord the "great commonwealth of Soviet nations" the benefit of "complete equality, of respect for territorial integrity, state independence and sovereignty, and of non-intervention in one another's internal affairs" and to recognize "the need for taking a full account of the historical past and peculiarities of each country that has taken the path of building a new life." [20] He also pointed out that Moscow's conduct was at variance with the Soviet-supported pro-

19. Soviet Intervention in Czechoslovakia: Secretary Rusk's News Conference, *ibid.,* pp. 261–63.
20. Legal Aspects of the Invasion and Occupation of Czechoslovakia; statements made on September 12, 1968, by U.S. Representative Herbert Reis in the U.N. Special Committee on Principles of International Law. United States, Department of State, *Bulletin,* LIX, October 14, 1968, p. 394; hereafter referred to as *Legal Aspects.*

vision in Articles 48 and 49 of the draft convention on the Law of Treaties [21] as well as with the 1965 General Assembly Declaration on the Inadmissibility of Intervention in the Domestic Affairs of States and the Protection of their Independence and Sovereignty, which guarantees each state the inalienable right to choose its own "political, economic, and social and cultural" system of government.[22]

Mr. Reis told his fellow committee members [23] that the new Soviet principles violated the "legal obligation" [24] of the U.N. Charter that "all Members shall refrain in their international relations from the threat or use of force against the territorial integrity or political independence of any state, or in any manner inconsistent with the Purposes of the United Nations." He emphasized that the charter makes only a very few specific exceptions to this rule. Article 51 does preserve the inherent right of individual or collective self-defense. But, Mr. Reis noted, "the fundamental condition precedent to exercise of the right of self-defense is an armed attack." [25] While the Soviet Union had alleged that an attack from the West and subversion from within

21. See, *ibid.,* p. 398. Draft Article 48 states: "The expression of a State's consent to be bound by a treaty which has been procured by the coercion of its representatives through acts or threat directed against him personally shall be without legal effect." Draft Article 49 states: "A treaty is void if its conclusion has been procured by the threat or use of force in violation of the principles of the Charter of the United Nations."
22. G. A. Res. 2131, U.N. Doc. A/6212, 20 U.N. GAOR, Supp. 14 at 11 (1965). The first principle of the declaration states: "No state has the right to intervene, directly or indirectly, for any reason whatsoever, in the internal or external affairs of any other state. Consequently, armed intervention and all other forms of interference or attempted threats against the personality of the state or against its political, economic and cultural elements, are condemned." Paragraph 5 states: "Every state has an inalienable right to choose its political, economic, and social and cultural systems, without interference in any form by any other state."
23. *Legal Aspects,* p. 394, US/UN Press Release 134.
24. *Ibid.,* p. 398.
25. *Ibid.,* p. 400.

were "imminent" in Czechoslovakia, no evidence was actually put forward, except for the discovery of one small arms cache in northwestern Bohemia.[26] Obviously such self-serving allegations, unless verified by proof acceptable to the international community, do not meet any legal standard for the use of force under Article 51. As for the dangers of subversion and counterrevolution, Mr. Reis emphasized that "the charter does not recognize any right of self-defense against 'counterrevolution.' No matter the intimacy of one country with another, neither may claim a right to invade the territory of its friend because of a threat of counterrevolution." [27]

The U.S. representative strongly rebutted the concept that a socialist "community" has special rights to act with force against a delinquent unable or unwilling to redress a situation regarded by the other members as a dereliction of the duties and norms of memberships. He reminded the committee that "the charter governs the relations between all member states, including Eastern European states. These countries are entitled to charter rights and the observance of charter duties in their relations among themselves. . . . From a legal point of view, there is no basis for asserting that the relationships of the Eastern European states among themselves are the concern of that group of states alone." [28]

Assumed in Mr. Reis's statements and other similar pronouncements by the U.S. is a belief in the strict legal efficacy and operative validity of the U.N. Charter's prohibitions on the unilateral use of force in interstate relations. Washington said that it was dismayed by Soviet violation of these norms and of the prevailing world sense of justice, and most of all by the idiosyncrasy of Soviet conduct. These views were echoed by others. The Rt. Hon. Michael Stewart, the British Foreign Secretary, said in Parliament on October 31, 1968, "nations have realized that what has happened in Czechoslovakia, and

26. *Ibid.*
27. *Ibid.*
28. *Ibid.*

what has been said by the Soviet Government since, brings into international affairs an alarming element of unpredictability. It would be a bold man or a fool who would like to make positive prophecies as to where next the policy of the Soviet Union might move. I say this particularly in view of Mr. Gromyko's statement about . . . the 'Socialist Commonwealth,' . . . that this concept had no geographical limits. We were left . . . with an assertion by the Soviet Union that it considers itself . . . entitled, if necessary, to invade the territory of other countries according to its judgment of where its and their interests lie." [29] According to Senator Jackson, chairman of the Senate Subcommittee on National Security and International Operations, "memories of August 1968 argue against any complacency that good sense will necessarily prevail in the decisions and actions of the Soviet Politburo." [30]

The Brezhnev Doctrine and related rhetoric of the Soviet Union was unanimously condemned by Western leaders for conducing to unpredictability and instability in international relations. In the words of Harlan Cleveland, the U.S. permanent representative to NATO, "The disturbing fact is that we do not really know what the Soviet leaders have in mind" when they advance these new principles, and that, consequently, "Soviet behavior must now be seen to be less predictable." [31] Thus the West began to detect in the Soviet behavior and rhetoric what Thomas Schelling [32] has rightly taught us to believe is the most

29. Great Britain. Parliament. House of Commons. *Parliamentary Debates* (Official Reports), Fifth Series, 772, col. 183, The Secretary of State for Foreign Affairs, Mr. Michael Stewart, October 31, 1968.
30. United States Senate, 91st Congress, 1st Session, *Czechoslovakia and the Brezhnev Doctrine,* prepared by the Subcommittee on National Security and International Operation, Committee on Government Operations (pursuant to Senate Res. 24, 91st Cong.), Washington, D.C.: U.S. Government Printing Office, 1969, p. 9.
31. Harlan Cleveland, "NATO After the Invasion," *Foreign Affairs,* 47, no. 2, January 1969, p. 251 at 256 and 259.
32. Thomas C. Schelling, *Arms and Influence,* New Haven: Yale University Press, 1966; hereafter referred to as *Arms and Influence.*

dangerous characteristic of state behavior: an absence of mutually shared behavior expectations and boundaries to guide the interaction of the superpowers. What the Russians had done in Czechoslovakia, and especially what they had said to explain what they were doing, was so far removed from the civilized rules of the game that suddenly all bets were off.

A natural response to such sudden uncertainty about the future intentions of a potentially dangerous neighbor is to oil one's rifle. According to *The New York Times,* the "Council of the North Atlantic Treaty Organization has recommended that, in the wake of the invasion of Czechoslovakia, all Western political and military policies be based on the unpredictability of Soviet behavior." [33] To this end, NATO resolved that its strength should be increased substantially: not so much because Soviet real power vis-à-vis the West has risen significantly as a result of the assault on one of its own allies but to be prepared for whatever lies ahead. Rearmament must achieve a level sufficient to deter any one of a number of Soviet policy options that we had previously thought excluded by self-imposed restraint reinforced by international custom and usage. Everything that a decade of *détente* and bridge building had seemed to make unthinkable the Brezhnev Doctrine now made vividly thinkable.

Not everyone treated the Brezhnev Doctrine as a bolt out of the blue. To some, it held little surprise. Mr. Dubcek's deposed Premier Oldrich Cernik sadly shrugged that the Czechoslovaks, however reluctantly, must accept their role as fixtures of a "new reality" in which "the basic platform for evaluating our activity

33. *The New York Times,* October 17, 1968, p. 5. NATO's performance during the actual Warsaw Pact invasion displayed appalling weakness. Szulc, for example, refers to the fact that despite the availability of much data-gathering equipment and installations, "NATO's communications network failed to function efficiently, and much vital information on the actual Soviet movements reached the responsible commanders only after considerable delay." Szulc claims that American military officers in Europe were "totally in the dark as to what was happening" and first learned of the invasion through announcements on Radio Prague; see Szulc, *op. cit.,* pp. 377–78.

from the international aspect must be the full respecting of the existence of two world systems and the fact that Czechoslovakia belongs to the socialist community." Czechoslovakia must adapt its "national interest" to that dominant fact.[34] In Paris, General De Gaulle contended that the Czechoslovak invasion, however deplorable, merely continued the "policy of blocs, which was imposed on Europe by the effects of [the] Yalta" agreements,[35] which France was working to end. Senator Eugene McCarthy, then campaigning for the Presidency, shocked many among his supporters by candidly saying much the same thing. To a grieving, outraged West, these discordant notes were embarrassing. The prevailing tendency was to treat them as malevolent, naive, cynical. After a field investigation, Senator Mike Mansfield reported to the Senate Foreign Relations Committee that the United States recognized no such "new reality" splitting the world into superpower spheres of predominance. "The rumors of 'deals' as between ourselves and the Soviet Union which would establish great power spheres have been refuted," he said. "There have been and there can be no agreements which would consign any of the independent nations of Eastern Europe to a permanent second-class status in relation to the Soviet Union." [36]

These shocked reactions and denials confirm the suspicion that our country has not cultivated the strategically important ability of listening to itself as if it were the enemy speaking.

34. *The New York Times,* October 19, 1968, p. 2.
35. *The New York Times,* August 22, 1968, p. 17. Interestingly, the Czechoslovaks were of a similar mind. Szulc, *op. cit.,* p. 401, writes, "The Czechs were and are convinced that at Yalta the world was divided into two spheres of influence—Soviet and American—and that it so remains." In protest against the West's obvious acceptance of the right of the Soviet Union to suppress Czechoslovakia, the people of Prague at the time of the invasion began to write on the city walls: MUNICH = YALTA.
36. United States Senate, 90th Congress, 2nd Session, *Postscript to Reports on Czechoslovakia, NATO, and the Paris Negotiations of September, 1968, Report of Senator Mike Mansfield to the Committee on Foreign Relations,* December 1968, Washington, D.C.: U.S. Government Printing Office, 1968, p. 5.

Cernik, De Gaulle, and McCarthy were all too right. The six principles of the Brezhnev Doctrine were each directly derived from our own verbal behavior in justifying U.S. policy toward the nations of the Western hemisphere. They introduced no norms and proposed no system transformations that were not already explicit in the official rhetoric of the United States during the Guatemalan, Cuban, and Dominican crises. They injected no new elements of unpredictability and evinced no new erratic or idiosyncratic tendencies in the Kremlin leaders that were not previously manifest in the pronouncements of our own spokesmen. No one listening to U.S. statements of policy during the Guatemalan, Cuban, and Dominican crises could have failed to conclude that we had already gone a long distance, at least verbally, toward consigning the nations of Latin America to permanent second-class status in our Western hemispheric "family." Implicit in what we did in Latin America between 1954 and 1965 and what we said to explain our conduct was the assumption that "we" had "our" region of enforced solidarity—and "they" had "theirs."

4

Limited Sovereignty
and the Inter-American System:
The Cases of Guatemala and Cuba

In the Guatemalan and Cuban crises, two small nations of the Western hemisphere sought to exert a sovereign will that was perceived by the United States as inimical to its essential self-interest and to the collective policy of the Americas. In both instances, the small state pursued military policies that introduced Communist weapons into Latin America. In both cases, the United States, and, with lesser enthusiasm, the Organization of American States, demanded an end to these policies and as a last resort used or facilitated the use of force to compel a change. The United States was successful in both instances. In the case of Guatemala, the leftist regime was replaced by a rightist one, which brought that country back into conformity with minimal U.S. and hemispheric standards of permissible conduct. In the case of Cuba, the missiles Havana had requested and obtained from the Soviet Union were summarily withdrawn by a U.S.-Soviet agreement to which Cuba was merely spectator.

These exploits thus represent triumphs of U.S. hemispheric policy. They are, however, more than merely isolated incidents, done, gone, and forgotten. As the United States acted to restrict the sovereignty of Guatemala and Cuba, it perforce set forth the principles governing its actions. It explained and justified its actions by employing a verbal strategy that placed acts in the context of broader principles. The acts themselves were fixed in time, but the principles the acts succeeded in manifesting were not. Inevitably, they became a part of the continuing system of interaction among states, and since the principles were being propounded by a superpower, they became part of the systemic relations of the superpowers.

The principles successfully put to work in the U.S. actions against Guatemala and Cuba became, by their very success, a part of the code of permissible conduct between a superpower and the states in its region. And they were not trivial, these principles we proclaimed and then succeeded in enforcing. It was the United States that first insisted on the right of a regional grouping to exclude the U.N. from intraregional disputes, on the right of the region to demand ideological conformity of its members, and to control aspects of these nations' domestic and foreign policies. That through our conduct these principles became or were confirmed as an acceptable way of international life, of relations between a great power and its smaller neighbors, is as much a part of the harvest of the Guatemalan and Cuban operations as was the overthrow of the Arbenz Guzman regime or the withdrawal of the Soviet missiles. These victories are the first-order consequences of U.S. strategy, and they are of great and immediate importance. But in appraising the costs and benefits of our strategy in these two crises it is essential also to keep in mind the second-order consequences, more subtle than the surface events but no less important to our national self-interest.

GUATEMALA

In mid-June 1954, began what *The New York Times* has subsequently described as "the CIA-engineered revolution against the

Communist-oriented President of Guatemala, Jacobo Arbenz Guzman." [1] A particular feature of this "revolution"—aside from the clandestine role of the United States—was the manner in which the regional system of the Americas was utilized to legitimate aggression against the Arbenz regime and to run interference against the United Nations.

Shortly before the commencement of the actual operation against Guatemala from bases in adjacent Nicaragua and Honduras—operations that included bombing of Guatemalan cities by American planes with American pilots [2]—the stage was set by the Tenth Inter-American Conference, which met at Caracas, Venezuela, from March 1 to 28, 1954. At this meeting of American foreign ministers, according to the State Department, "one of the principal objectives of the United States delegation . . . headed by Secretary Dulles, was to achieve maximum agreement among the American Republics upon a clear-cut and unmistakable policy determination against the intervention of international communism in the hemisphere, recognizing the continuing threat which it poses to their peace and security and declaring their intention to take effective measures, individually and collectively, to combat it." [3] These sentiments were incorporated in a resolution from which Mexico and Argentina abstained, and which Guatemala understandably opposed.

Here for the first time we encounter an expansion of the notion that communism, as an alien theology, constitutes aggression against the entire inter-American system whenever and wherever it appears in the Western hemisphere and that the American states have a duty to take collective and individual measures to defend the system against it. The doublethink runs like this: communism is aggression. Therefore an attack on Guatemala is self-defense if it saves the Guatemalan people from their own leftist

1. *The New York Times* series on CIA Operations, April 28, 1966, p. 28.
2. *Ibid.*
3. William G. Bowdler, "Report on the Tenth Inter-American Conference," United States, Department of State, *Bulletin,* XXX, April 26, 1954, p. 634.

regime. The argument by now has a familiar ring. At the time, however, the idea of a large nation "taking measures" against a smaller "in self-defense" was not a way of thinking widely associated with the United States. Nevertheless, we find the Inter-American Conference determining "that international communism, by its anti-democratic nature and its interventionist tendency, is incompatible with the concept of American freedom," that "the activities of the international communist movement" constitute "intervention in American affairs," and that these communist activities are invariably pursued "in the interests of an alien despotism." In the light of these sweeping presumptions it was decided that "the domination or control of the political institutions of any American State by the international communist movement, extending to this hemisphere the political system of an extracontinental power, would constitute a threat to the sovereignty and political independence of the American States, endangering the peace of America. . . ." [4]

With this U.S.-initiated declaration, a new principle asserted itself in postwar international relations. This principle holds that a regional organization may designate a particular sociopolitical ideology as alien to the region. Thus it may act collectively in ideological self-defense of regional conformity. But the Americas were not the only region in which a superpower and its ideology were preponderant. Such a principle could scarcely be insisted upon by one superpower's regional organization without also being insisted upon by the other's.

Since Guatemala at that time was the only American state accused by the United States of communism, there was not much question whom the declaration had in mind when it contemplated "appropriate action in accordance with existing treaties." [5] To remove any lingering doubt, the U.S. Senate on June 25, 1954, at

---

4. Declaration of Solidarity for the Preservation of the Political Integrity of the American States Against International Communist Intervention, *ibid.,* p. 638.
5. *Ibid.*

the actual time of the so-called Guatemalan "revolution," passed Concurrent Resolution 91. This found "strong evidence of intervention by the international Communist movement in the State of Guatemala, whereby government institutions have been infiltrated by Communist agents, weapons of war have been secretly shipped into that country, and the pattern of Communist conquest has become manifest. . . ." [6] The term "conquest" in this context is particularly significant, as no overt change in Guatemalan government had occurred since 1944 [7] and no foreign bases or troops had been located there.

It is striking to note how exactly these allegations parallel those of the Warsaw Pact nations' charges against the Czechoslovak leaders in 1968: that the infiltration of reactionary elements into the Czechoslovak government, the mass media and the party "threatens . . . to push your country from the road of socialism, and thereby threatens the interests of the entire socialist system." [8] The Soviets, too, declared that Western weapons of war had been infiltrated into Czechoslovakia,[9] and that "anti-socialist and revisionist forces have gained control over the press, radio and television. . . ." [10]

What matters, however, is not whether the allegations made in Concurrent Resolution 91 were true or those contained in the Warsaw Letter were false. The nub of the matter is, surely, whether *any* regional system should have the right to require nations in the region to conform to its norms on pain of having its national devi-

6. Text of Senate Concurrent Resolution 91 of June 25, 1954. United States, Department of State, *Bulletin*, XXXI, July 5, 1954, p. 29; also, Congressional Resolution 91, 83rd Congress, 2d Session, 100 Congressional Record 8921 (1954).
7. Cf., Samuel Guy Inman and W. Donald Beatty, "Guatemala," Collier's *Encyclopedia*, Vol. 11, New York: Crowell-Collier Publishing Company, 1965, pp. 490–99, esp. 497.
8. Warsaw Letter sent by the Five Warsaw Pact leaders to the Czechoslovak Communist National Committee, Warsaw, July 18, 1968, *The Times* of London, July 19, 1968, p. 8.
9. *The New York Times*, July 20, 1968, pp. 1–2.
10. Warsaw Letter, *supra*.

ation judged by other states in the family, then treated as an act of "aggression" against the system, and, finally, eradicated by regional "collective self-defense." Congress and the Caracas Conference came close for the first time to answering that question affirmatively. While U.S. rhetoric may have been intended to do no more than express hostility to Guatemala or to pave the way for the CIA operation against its government, the actual verbal strategy went much further. It signaled our willingness in principle to live in a world system of ideologically orthodox, superpower-dominated regional blocs or "ghettos." As we shall see, this consequence of what we said and did is not dependent on whether it was intended, but is inherent in the nature of the international system.

The Guatemalan "revolution" caused us to propound another important principle. In those days of June 1954, there arose the first occasion to test in practice the uneasy balance between regional and world organization. As soon as hostilities had begun, Guatemala, despite an earlier tentative approach to the Organization of American States, appealed to the United Nations Security Council for observers to investigate the source of the aggression.[11] The United States representative, Mr. Lodge, together with other OAS states' representatives on the Security Council, took a firm— and successful—line in preventing this. They steadfastly insisted that the Guatemalan complaint was "precisely the kind of problem which, in the first instance, should be dealt with on an urgent basis by an appropriate agency of the Organization of American States." [12]

In view of the position taken by the members of that organization just previously at Caracas, it is not surprising that Guatemala continued to clamor for U.N. action as the invasion

---

11. Cf., cablegram dated 19 June 1954 from the Minister for External Relations of Guatemala addressed to the President of the Security Council, U.N. Doc. S/3232, 19 June 1954; also, letter dated 22 June 1954 from the Representative of Guatemala addressed to the Secretary-General, U.N. Doc. S/3241, 23 June 1954.

12. H. C. Lodge, SCOR, IX, 675th Mtg., p. 29.

by Col. Castillo Armas' U.S.-supported and Nicaraguan-based army proceeded apace. The American states, however, were successful in keeping the dispute bottled up in the Inter-American Peace Committee of the OAS until the Arbenz Guzman government had collapsed. In the solicitous words of the Turkish representative, "The situation . . . in Guatemala may be likened to a family misunderstanding. And family misunderstandings can often best be solved, first of, all, by the family's own members. To try to seek other means can only complicate and delay the solution of the problem." [13] He also reminded the council that "in this troubled world we badly need [the] solidarity" a regional system fosters.[14]

This was a position with which the United States was only too happy to agree. Ambassador Lodge warned that a balance between regionalism and universalism had been struck at San Francisco, that only because such a balance had been achieved did the Senate ratify the U.N. Charter, and that U.S. membership in the organization rested on the implementation of that balance. Defining it at the time of the Guatemala crisis, however, Mr. Lodge preferred the balance to be one tilted sharply toward regional pre-eminence in disputes between members of the regional system. He noted the determination of the American states "that the United Nations should be supplementary to and not a substitute for or impairment of the tried and trusted regional relationships. . . ." [15] Darkly he added that "if the United Nations Security Council does not respect the right of the Organization of American States to achieve a pacific settlement of the dispute between Guatemala and its neighbours, the result will be a catastrophe of such dimensions as will gravely impair the future effectiveness both of the United Nations itself and of regional organizations such as the Organization of American States." [16] As for Soviet efforts to have the U.N.

---

13. O. Derinsu, SCOR, IX, 676th Mtg., p. 18.
14. *Ibid.*
15. H. C. Lodge, SCOR, IX, 676th Mtg., p. 28.
16. *Ibid.*, pp. 28–29.

look into the matter, by sending observers, this was like a stranger rummaging through our family affairs. Ambassador Lodge declared, "I say to the representative of the Soviet Union, stay out of this hemisphere and do not try to start your plans and your conspiracies over here." [17] The region, the United States was saying to Russia, is ours and we will tolerate no interference from outside, not even through the agency of the U.N.

The very fact, however, that the Guatemalan operation was carried on primarily by Guatemalans, albeit backed by the resources of the United States, and that the U.S. involvement and that of other American states was carefully hidden from view does indicate that the American states were not ready to advocate openly the principle that they could individually or collectively use military force to remove or restrict the sovereignty of an "alien interventionist" regime within the region. In the Cuban case, however, the U.S. did exactly that.

CUBA

By the time the United States confronted Cuba over the Russian missiles in 1962, the modesty, conscience, or concern for U.N. principles that had led Washington to act covertly in the case of Guatemala had given way to a willingness to employ military forces openly in the naval quarantine.

To understand this aspect of the Cuban crisis, it is necessary to take into account the intervening events of the Hungarian and Suez crises of 1956. These two monumental events had a profound effect—perhaps *too* profound—on the subsequent strategic thinking of the United States.

In the Suez crisis, the United States adhered strictly to the principles of the U.N. Charter, even at heavy cost to the unity of NATO and to Franco-American relations in particular. In Secretary Dulles' words, the use of force by Britain, France, and

17. H. C. Lodge, SCOR, IX, 675th Mtg., p. 32.

Israel, allies all of the United States, "involves principles which far transcend the immediate issue. . . ." [18] If we were to admit that states, including our allies, even under great provocation by Egypt, could use force to redress their grievances, it would mean that "the principle of renunciation of force is no longer respected and that there still exists the right whenever a nation feels itself subject to injustice to resort to force. . . ." Then, "we would have, I fear, torn this [U.N.] charter into shreds and the world would again be a world of anarchy." [19]

Dulles, of course, was not acting purely altruistically. His adherence to U.N. principles was a strategy of self-interest, one based on the existence of a system with rules of conduct applying equally to all the players in the game, including the superpowers. The Hungarian crisis, which ran virtually parallel to the Suez crisis, disproved the existence of any such effective system of rules. Not only did it turn out that the Russians were not playing by the same rules, but the neutral states in the U.N. proved notably reluctant to blame Moscow for its default or to try to do anything about it. Krishna Menon of India pretended to see the rape of Hungary as a very minor infraction, comparable to the merest lapse in democratic process: "We cannot say that a sovereign member of this Assembly . . . can be called upon to submit its elections and everything else to the United Nations. . . ." [20] The Hungarian bodies crushed under the treads of Soviet tanks were not, however, merely stopped from voting.

The parallel events of 1956—Suez and Hungary—and the unparallel way in which they developed thus appeared to demonstrate to Washington that the United States had surrendered a potential Western advantage by adhering to the principles of the Charter and forcing its allies back; while the Soviets, at little cost even in world prestige, had scored a gain by blatantly violating

18. Statement by Secretary Dulles in the General Assembly. United States, Department of State, *Bulletin,* XXXV, November 12, 1956, p. 751.
19. *Ibid.,* p. 752.
20. 571 U.N. GAOR 68 (II Emer. Special Session 1956).

those same principles. Although there had been widespread disapproval of the Soviet invasion of Hungary among people and states, there were inevitably those in U.S. policy-making positions who felt that the episode had demonstrated that the U.N. and the so-called third world had neither the power nor the moral integrity to mount an effective defense of the principles of the Charter.

It is possible, however, that U.S. strategists may have been too eager to bring their country's *realpolitik* into line with what appeared to be the lesson of Hungary. The destruction of Hungarian independence may be seen in retrospect as the last in the chain of postwar Stalinist suppressions. In the ensuing years, as part of the process of de-Stalinization, Moscow appears to have been trying to backpedal. The Kadar regime turned out to be less repressive than had been feared. The declaration of twelve Communist parties in November 1957 asserted with Soviet concurrence that the "socialist countries base their relations on the principles of complete equality, respect for territorial integrity and state independence and sovereignty, and noninterference in one another's affairs." In November 1960 the declaration of eighty-one Communist parties reiterated that "every country in the socialist camp is ensured genuine equality of rights and independence." According to the Jackson subcommittee of the U.S. Senate, by then the idea of "different roads to socialism had become respectable in discussions between the Soviet Union and its Warsaw Pact allies." [21] In Eastern Europe there already was considerable nonconformist experimentation in land ownership, industrial decentralization, widening of party membership, official attitude toward non-Communists, incentive pay, relaxation of censorship, right to travel, and administration of justice. By the early 1960's the Hungarian invasion was becoming widely regarded, in Eastern Europe as in the West, as the last death rattle of Stalinism—an anachronism in the fifties, inconceivable in the sixties.[22]

21. *Czechoslovakia and the Brezhnev Doctrine, supra,* p. 2.
22. Notably, the Soviets' justification for the invasion of Hungary both emulated the principles the United States had enunciated during the Guatemalan crisis and anticipated the Brezhnev Doctrine. In the

By the end of the sixties, however, Hungarian-style invasion was evidently again conceivable. For this, the principles upon which the United States fashioned its policies toward Latin America in the first half of the sixties cannot escape a measure of responsibility.

Castro posed—and poses—to the United States a problem not only of major international, but also of domestic, political consequence. At first, the United States tried to deal with this new problem as it had with Arbenz Guzman—by covert direct intervention. Covertness was carefully planned and executed. In July 1960, at the Security Council, U.S. Ambassador Henry Cabot Lodge stated categorically (and, alas, as far as he knew, no doubt truthfully): "The Foreign Minister of Cuba has told us that Dr. Castro would like an assurance from the United States that the United States has no aggressive purposes against Cuba. Unneces-

words of Ambassador Sobolev, "Soviet forces . . . are helping to put an end to the counter-revolutionary intervention and riots; the presence of Soviet forces in Hungary serves the common interest of the security of all the countries parties to the Pact. It was a measure taken to counter the militarization of Western Germany. . . ." Ambassador Sobolev, SCOR, XI, Mtg. 754, 4 Nov. 1956, p. 10. The Soviet position generally confirmed the OAS argument that a regional grouping is permanent and immutable and that its interests and ideology are determined by the grouping as a whole. It confirmed that any deviation from that norm by, or in, one of the states that have belonged to the system constitutes an "intervention." In the Hungarian instance this "intervention" was by "international forces of reaction and counter-revolution" against which "collective action" may be taken by the system in "self-defense." Just as did the OAS and the United States in the instance of Guatemala, so now the Warsaw Pact states and the Soviet Union could determine for themselves that an intervention had occurred, citing evidence of the incursion into high places of government and popular media of persons serving an alien ideology, as well as such evidence of intervention as the infiltration of foreign agents, weapons, and the dissemination of hostile propaganda by foreign broadcasters:

"It is known that the forces of reaction within the country were acting in close contact with international reaction, and immediately after the armed putsch was started they were receiving effective aid from the west. . . . According to Italian press reports . . . detach-

sary though it most certainly seems to me, let me here and now give him this assurance, heaped up and overflowing: the United States has no aggressive purpose against Cuba." [23] What made Ambassador Lodge's eloquent assurance so poignant is that it was given at a time when U.S. planning was already well into the now-familiar exercise: training émigré battalions, overpainting U.S. insignias on sea and air craft, in short, wholly committing itself to the covert Bay of Pigs operation.[24]

The lesson Havana learned from the Bay of Pigs was that its powerful neighbor would probably, in various increasingly direct ways, continue to seek to infringe its sovereignty. The lesson Washington learned was that covertness could be a crucial handicap. When Cuba attempted to take its fears of a new, more direct U.S. intervention to the Security Council, the United States, far from disavowing hostile intentions, steadfastly replied that "recourse of

ments of Hungarian Fascist émigrés who served in Horthy's army in the past, crossed into Hungary from Western Germany, via Austria. They were armed with American weapons. . . . According to official information of the Hungarian Government, 30 airplanes arrived from Austria on Nov. 2nd; a further 70 planes arrived on Nov. 3rd; they brought considerable amount of munitions in boxes marked with the Red Cross and persons who acted as the organizers of the counter-revolutionary revolt. . . . That promise of armed intervention on the part of the Western powers in the internal affairs of the Hungarian state was reinforced by the campaign for the recruitment of volunteers started in a number of countries. . . ." Pavel Baranikov, correspondent of *Izvestia*, "What Happened in Hungary," November 1956, pp. 26–28. "Energetic preparations for overthrowing the people's democratic system in Hungary and in other East European countries, have been conducted in the United States of America, for example, for many years. . . . Along with those supplies, the planes (Red Cross) brought men in white smocks, but we could see well the military uniforms under those smocks. . . ." *The Truth About Hungary,* Moscow: Foreign Languages Publishing House, 1957, pp. 7–17. For a book containing worldwide documentary reaction, see M. Lasky, *The Hungarian Revolution,* London: Martin Secker and Warburg, Ltd., 1957.

23. SCOR, XV, 874th Mtg., 18 July 1960, p. 27.

24. Arthur M. Schlesinger, Jr., *A Thousand Days: John F. Kennedy in The White House,* Boston: Houghton Mifflin, 1965, pp. 222, 226–29.

the Cuban Government to the Security Council . . . is not in harmony with its treaty obligations under the Inter-American Treaty of Reciprocal Assistance signed at Rio de Janeiro on 2 September 1947 and the Charter of the Organization of American States signed at Bogota on 30 April 1948." [25] Yet in the same speech Ambassador Lodge noted that the OAS was itself a complainant against Castro. The principles of the Monroe Doctrine, Lodge noted, "are now embodied in treaty obligations among the American States and in the Rio de Janeiro Treaty, which provide means for common action to prevent the establishment of a regime dominated by international communism in the Western Hemisphere." [26] Thus Cuba stood condemned by the regional organization, threatened with "common action" by the region, but precluded by the regional system from taking its dispute to the U.N. The United States was thus again demanding that the wayward canary be judged by the community of cats.

The insistence of the United States on referring the Cuban complaint to the OAS led Ambassador Sobolev to a logically impeccable conclusion: "That proposal means that the question of aggressive acts by the United States would be transferred to a body in which the United States has a predominating influence and could quietly deal with Cuba as it pleased." [27] The United States was determined, however, to keep its dispute with Cuba in the OAS and out of the Security Council. In pursuing this objective, the State Department worked to reinforce the principle of hemispheric solidarity. It persuaded the OAS foreign ministers' meeting at San José to proclaim in August 1960 "that all members of the regional organization are under obligation to submit to the discipline of the Inter-American system, voluntarily and freely agreed upon. . . ." [28]

25. H. C. Lodge, SCOR, XV, 874th Mtg., 18 July 1960, p. 27.
26. *Ibid.,* p. 32.
27. V. P. Sobolev, SCOR, XV, 876th Mtg., 19 July 1960, pp. 15–16.
28. OAS Official Records, OEA/SER. F/11.7; U.N. Doc. S/4480, Declaration of San José, Costa Rica, 29 August 1960, Final Act of the Seventh Meeting of Consultation of Ministers of Foreign Affairs, pp. 5–6.

At the Punta del Este meeting of the Organ of Consultation in January 1962, convoked at U.S. initiative under Article 6 of the Rio Treaty, the content of this "discipline" was spelled out. The "adherence by any member of the Organization of American States to Marxism-Leninism is incompatible with the Inter-American system and the alignment of such a government with the communist bloc breaks the unity and solidarity of the hemisphere." [29] Specifically, it was "decided" that "the present Government of Cuba, which has officially identified itself as a Marxist-Leninist government, is incompatible with the principles and objectives of the Inter-American system. . . ." [30] Then, having reiterated the right of the American "family" to set norms of conduct for its members, and after reiterating the Guatemala norm outlawing "alien" Marxism-Leninism from the hemisphere, the "family" proceeded at the ninth meeting of the Organ of Consultation in July 1962 to apply sanctions against Cuba in accordance with articles 6 and 8 of the Rio Treaty. The ninth meeting, acting on the report of a committee to investigate charges of "intervention and aggression" by Cuba against Venezuela—a committee whose findings may well have been correct but which could scarcely pass the test of impartiality—decided that the governments of the American states should not maintain diplomatic or consular relations with Cuba, should suspend all trade except in foodstuffs, medicines, and medical equipment, and should discontinue all sea transport except as may be required for humanitarian purposes.[31] With this resolution, the Organ of Consultation proclaimed the regional system's right to employ coercive measures against one of its members. This action is all the more striking since it purports to exercise the disciplinary power of the organization against a state that had already been suspended at the preceding meeting of the Organ

29. Inter-American Treaty of Reciprocal Assistance, Applications, Vol. 1, 1948–59, Pan-American Union, General Secretariat, Washington, D.C., Part One, Resolution II of the Eighth Meeting of Consultation, Punta del Este, Uruguay, January, 1962, p. 9; U.N. Doc. S/5075.
30. *Ibid.*
31. Ninth Meeting of Consultation, Washington, D.C., July 21–26, 1962, Resolution I, *ibid.,* p. 10.

of Consultation. Such dramatic application of sanctions must be seen against the background of Article 53 of the U.N. Charter, which establishes that "no enforcement action shall be taken under regional arrangement or by regional agencies without the authorization of the Security Council. . . ." The United States had openly committed itself to the principle that regional arrangements take precedence over the commitments in the U.N. Charter even though, in ratifying the charter, we had subscribed (Article 103) to exactly the opposite rule.

It should again be noted that the principles by which the United States chose to activate the OAS were not forced upon it by circumstances, but represent a policy choice. The United States could have sought simply to indict Cuba as an aggressor against Venezuela or an exporter of revolution. For both these contentions there was considerable evidence. We chose, however, to emphasize Cuba's ideological nonconformity and to brand *that* as aggression per se. The strategy of the State Department was to emphasize the illegality not of what Cuba was *doing* so much as of what Cuba *was;* not so much of Cuban *aggressiveness* as of Cuban *communism*. No doubt it was the underlying belief that communism invariably breeds aggressiveness. But was it to our interest to establish a conclusive presumption of this sort? Did we stop to consider that the other side could similarly establish its conclusive presumptions and then claim the same right as we to use coercion against the presumed, rather than proven, realities?

The culmination of the use of coercive sanctions against the deviant Havana regime was prompted by the Soviet deployment of nuclear missiles on Cuban soil. In any examination of principles pertaining to the right to use force, President Kennedy's speech of October 22 requires particularly close study. It is an emphatic assertion of a regional grouping's right to determine, without U.N. "interference," when its self-interest requires the use of military force for coercive purposes.[32]

The United States justified the Cuban quarantine and im-

32.   Robert F. Kennedy, *Thirteen Days: A Memoir of the Cuban Missile Crisis,* New York: W. W. Norton, 1969, p. 31, comments, "Most

posed its demand for the removal of Soviet missiles by reference
to five principles:

1. *Cuba, as a nation belonging to the American bloc, cannot escape the jurisdiction of that bloc.* According to President
Kennedy, Cuba is " . . . in an area well known to have a special
and historical relationship to the United States and the nations of
the Western Hemisphere. . . ." [33] The OAS foreign ministers con-
currently declared that "The Inter-American system is based on
consistent adherence by its constituent states to certain objectives
and principles of solidarity, set forth in the instruments that gov-
ern it; among these objectives and principles are . . . rejection of
alliances and agreements that may lead to intervention in America
by extra-continental powers." [34] The requirement of "consistent
adherence" to the rules of the regional bloc, we said, are obligatory even for a state like Cuba which preferred to be independent
of the bloc. Bloc loyalty, we contended, is a requirement dictated
by geography and history not by the self-determined preference of
any individual nation. Should accidents of geography determine
the fate of states—any more than accidents of birth should determine that of a person? The United States clearly went on record
answering yes to this question.

2. *The bloc may impose its norms on Cuba.* According to
President Kennedy " . . . the nations of this hemisphere decided

[of the executive committee of the National Security Council] felt,
at that stage, that an air strike against the missile sites could be
the only course. Listening to the proposals, I passed a note to the
President: 'I now know how Tojo felt when he was planning Pearl
Harbor.' "

33. United States. National Archives, *Public Papers of the Presidents of
the United States, John F. Kennedy: Containing the Public Messages, Speeches, and Statements of the President, January 1 to
December 31, 1962, Washington, D.C.: U.S.G.P.O., 1963,* "Radio
and Television Report to the American People on the Soviet Arms
Buildup in Cuba," October 22, 1962, pp. 806–09, at p. 807; hereafter referred to as *Public Papers (JFK).*
34. Resolution VI of the Eighth Meeting of Consultation of the
American Foreign Ministers, January, 1962. United States, Department of State, *Bulletin,* XLVI, 1962, p. 281.

long ago against the military presence of outside powers" in this area.[35] Moreover, the importation of "large, long-range, and clearly offensive weapons of sudden mass destruction—constitutes an explicit threat to the peace and security of all the Americas, in flagrant and deliberate defiance of the Rio Pact of 1947, the traditions of this Nation and hemisphere, the joint resolution of the 87th Congress, the Charter of the United Nations, and my own public warnings to the Soviets on September 4 and 13." [36] At the time, it should be noted, none of these was binding on Cuba except the U.N. Charter. The statement implicitly postulates a limitation on Cuban sovereignty based on its geography and history as part of the American "family." Kennedy particularly castigated the secrecy with which these weapons had been installed, noting that the "foreign ministers of the OAS, in their communiqué of October 6, rejected secrecy on such matters in this hemisphere." [37] The position suggests that a sovereign state within our sphere of primacy must always have its books open to our inspection and may not keep secrets from us. Cuba's offenses against the American system were, it seems, twofold—receiving Soviet missiles and receiving them secretly.

3. *It is the United States or its bloc which determines whether the norms set by it have been complied with by Cuba.* On September 13, 1962, President Kennedy stated in reply to a question whether he had set any rule or standard for the application of the Monroe Doctrine to Cuba, "Well, I have indicated that if Cuba should possess a capacity to carry out offensive actions against the United States, that the United States would act." [38] In other words, it is for the United States to determine whether a state within its bloc may possess, or have stationed on its soil, weapons of a capability comparable to those possessed

35. *Public Papers (JFK)*, p. 808.
36. *Ibid.,* p. 806.
37. *Ibid.,* p. 808.
38. "The President's News Conference of September 13, 1962," *ibid.,* pp. 674–81, at p. 675.

by the United States and even stationed by the United States in foreign countries that feel the need for such protection. In his address of October 22, moreover, President Kennedy judged Cuba to have violated a rule laid down for it by the U.S. Congress in joint resolution. This resolution determined, in part, that "whereas the international Communist movement has increasingly extended into Cuba its political, economic, and military sphere of influence . . . the United States is determined (a) to prevent by whatever means may be necessary, including the use of arms, the Marxist-Leninist regime in Cuba from extending, by force or the threat of force, its aggressive or subversive activities to any part of this hemisphere; (b) to prevent in Cuba the creation or use of an externally supported military capability endangering the security of the United States." [39] A similar finding of deviation from the established norms is contained in the OAS Council's resolution of October 23 which states that "incontrovertible evidence has appeared that the Government of Cuba, despite repeated warnings, has secretly endangered the peace of the continent by permitting the Sino-Soviet powers to have intermediate and middle-range missiles on its territory capable of carrying nuclear warheads. . . ." [40] "These steps," the council went on, "are far in excess of any conceivable defense requirements of Cuba." [41] The regional grouping has thus asserted its right to decide on the sufficiency of the defense requirements of states within the region.

4. *If the members of the bloc determine that Cuba is in dereliction of its duty to abide by the norms established by the bloc, then force may be used to secure the necessary compliance. The use of force in such circumstances is not aggression but collective self-defense.* In addition to proclaiming his quarantine and

39. Joint Congressional Resolution Expressing the Determination of the United States with Respect to Cuba. United States, Department of State, *Bulletin*, XLVII, 1962, p. 597.
40. OAS Doc. OEA/SER.G/111, C - sa - 463, Resolution of the Council of the OAS of October 23, 1962; United States, Department of State, *Bulletin*, XLVII, 1962, p. 723.
41. Resolution of the Council of the OAS of October 23, 1962, *ibid.*

calling "an immediate meeting of the Organ of Consultation under the Organization of American States, to consider this threat to hemispheric security," [42] the President told the Cuban people that "your leaders are no longer Cuban leaders inspired by Cuban ideals. They are puppets and agents of an international conspiracy which has turned Cuba against your friends and neighbors in the Americas. . . ." [43] In other words, if a regime deviates from regional conformity, it thereby forfeits the rights to which a sovereign government is otherwise entitled. In view of Cuba's violations of the norms set for her by the United States and by the Inter-American bloc, it was thus appropriate for the Council of the OAS to recommend that its members "take all measures, individually and collectively, including the use of armed force, which they may deem necessary to ensure that the government of Cuba cannot continue to receive from the Sino-Soviet powers military material and related supplies. . . ." [44] These measures included a sea blockade, which in U.S. officials' terminology "involved the use of naval force to interfere with shipping on the high seas." [45] The blockade effectively restrained the exercise by two sovereign states, Cuba and the Soviet Union, of their right to choose the means by which to cooperate in military matters. It was, however, defended by the United States as an act both of "anticipatory" self-defense [46] and as collective regional action short of actual enforcement.[47] Abram Chayes, then the State Department's chief legal adviser, declared "the Soviet missiles in Cuba were a threat to the security of the United States and the Western Hemisphere. As such they endangered the peace of the world." [48] Chayes went further, citing a new version of the U.N. Charter in support of the U.S. initiative. Writ-

42. *Public Papers (JFK)*, p. 808.
43. *Ibid.,* p. 809.
44. Resolution VI of the Eighth Meeting of Consultation, *ibid.,* p. 281.
45. Abram Chayes, "Law and the Quarantine of Cuba," 41 *Foreign Affairs* 550 (1963), p. 550.
46. A. Stevenson, SCOR, XVII, 1025th Mtg., 25 October 1962, p. 4.
47. Abram Chayes, Legal Adviser, Department of State, Proceedings of the American Society of International Law, 57th Annual Meeting, Washington, D.C., April 25–27, 1963, p. 10, at p. 12.
48. Chayes, *loc. cit.,* p. 550.

ing in *Foreign Affairs,* he said, "The Charter obligation to refrain from the use of force is not absolute. Article 51, of course, affirms that nothing in the Charter impairs 'the inherent right of individual or collective self-defense.' " [49] In so stating, Chayes was engaging in some significant informal amending of the actual text of the charter. By inserting a period and ending the reference to Article 51 before the last and inconvenient phrase which actually limits the right of self-defense *to a case of an armed attack,* the rhetorical basis was laid for a new principle of international conduct or the return to an old one, which permits each state to use force against another whenever it deems its interests threatened, rather than only when it has actually been the victim of a genuine act of aggression.

Ambassador Stevenson strove to show that the quarantine was a genuine case of self-defense. He asserted that a "peril" had been posed to the security of the United States "because the Soviet Union has extended its nuclear threat into the Western Hemisphere." [50] Under the circumstances, he argued, there was no choice but for the Americas to act against anticipated Cuban or Soviet-Cuban aggression: "Were we," Ambassador Stevenson demanded, "to do nothing until the knife was sharpened? Were we to stand idly by until it was at our throats?" [51] This was a threat "which the American Republics are entitled to meet, as they have done, by appropriate regional defensive methods." [52]

The attempt to prove the imminence of an actual Soviet-Cuban nuclear missile attack was not, however, particularly convincing. President Kennedy himself, in his address of October 22, had noted candidly that Soviet missiles had for some time before already been effectively deployed to strike at American cities. "American citizens," he said, "have become adjusted to living daily on the bulls'-eye of Soviet missiles located inside the U.S.S.R. or in submarines." [53]

49. *Ibid.,* p. 554.
50. SCOR, XVII, 1025th Mtg., 25 October 1962, p. 2.
51. *Ibid.,* p. 4.
52. *Ibid.,* p. 5.
53. *Public Papers (JFK),* p. 807.

It was thus extraordinarily difficult to devise a principle that would permit the United States to use force against Russia and Cuba in this instance while yet retaining a normative standard of conduct that would effectively impose at least some limits on the right of states in general to revert to force. Some officials and advisers simply gave up the task. "The power, position and prestige of the United States had been challenged by another state," Dean Acheson explained, "and law simply does not deal with such questions of ultimate power. . . ." [54]

5. *The expansion of an alien communist ideology into the American family will be tolerated only within strict limits which the family itself sets and which it may impose with force on a deviating member of the family.* Ambassador Stevenson himself, in his opening statement before the Security Council on October 23, drew this principle to the attention of the world community:

> For 150 years the nations of the Americas have painfully labored to construct a hemisphere of independent and cooperating nations, free from foreign threats. An international system far older than this [U.N.] one—the Inter-American system—has been erected on this principle. The principle of the territorial integrity of the Western Hemisphere has been woven into the history, the life, and the thought of all the people of the Americas. In striking at that principle the Soviet Union is striking at the strongest and most enduring strain in the policy of this hemisphere. It is disrupting the convictions and aspirations of a century and a half. It is intruding on the firm policies of twenty nations. To allow this challenge to go unanswered would be to undermine a basic and historic pillar of the security of this hemisphere. [55]

These five points exactly anticipate those of the Brezhnev Doctrine.

54. Dean Acheson, Proceedings of the American Society of International Law, 57th Annual Meeting, Washington, D.C., April 25–27, 1963, p. 14.
55. A. Stevenson, SCOR, XVII, 1022nd Mtg., 23 October 1962, p. 12.

Although the precise circumstances of the Cuban missile crisis and the Czechoslovakian crisis of 1968 are, of course, different, the entire verbal conceptualization of American and OAS positions during the missile crisis unmistakably makes the principles of the Brezhnev Doctrine seem more reciprocal than innovative.

The sixth point of the Brezhnev Doctrine is that the bloc may not only use coercive force to compel the deviant state to adhere to bloc norms but may specifically extend coercion to include the use of armed force to invade the deviant's territory and reconstitute its government in order to reestablish conformity. This farthest-reaching of the six principles finds no support in the language of the United States and the OAS at the time of the confrontation with Cuba and the Soviet Union in 1962. President Kennedy firmly rebuffed the attempts of advisers to settle the missile crisis by a military attack.[56] But the same restraint was not shown by President Johnson during the crisis over the Dominican Republic.

56. Cf., R. F. Kennedy, *op. cit.*, esp. pp. 33–43.

5

The Johnson Doctrine

It appears that two determinations underlay each of the instances in which unilateral force was used by a superpower within its "region": (1) a unilateral finding of fact and (2) a unilateral decision about how that fact affected its national self-interest. These two determinations are likely to be interactive. The more dangerous to U.S. self-interest hemispheric communism is seen to be, the more hemispheric communism is likely to be perceived lurking behind each crisis. In crucial matters of national self-interest, diplomats and leaders tend to overreact, to take no chances that could redound against their country or against their careers. No one gets fired from the State Department, according to conventional wisdom, for *over*perceiving the Communist threat in a crisis, but a number of careers have been wrecked by underestimating it. The equivalent, no doubt, is true of the Soviets. This does not mean that our officials were deliberately distorting the truth in their reporting and assessment of the events that preceded hemispheric interventions in Guatemala, Cuba, and the Dominican Republic or, for that matter, in the extrahemispheric U.S. interventions in Lebanon, Stanleyville, and Vietnam. Neither, however, is there cause to doubt the genuineness of the Soviet leaders who thought they saw capitalist counterrevolutionaries gaining control in Budapest and Prague. We each perceive through the filter of our subjectivity—and our subjectivity inclines us to expect and to perceive the worst where "world communism" or "the world capitalist conspiracy" is concerned.

Genuineness or sincerity are, however, poor substitutes for objectivity. Unfortunately the international order has devised no system that requires a superpower to check its policymakers' unilateral perceptions of fact against those of others with different perceptive "sets" in order to gain perspective and more objectivity. But what the international orders did devise at San Francisco in 1945, was a limit on the right of states to react *with force* to such unilaterally perceived facts. The U.N. Charter is a treaty obliging its 126 signatory states to refrain from the threat or use of force in their relations with each other and to use armed force only in self-defense against an armed attack or, when duly authorized, by way of collective enforcement action by the United Nations itself. The "armed attack" standard is one deliberately chosen because it permits fairly clear, objective testing; immediately after hostilities have begun a quick look at the battle map will usually establish beyond reasonable doubt exactly who attacked whom. In all instances other than an armed attack, the use of military force is clearly prohibited. It is this limitation that has now been discarded by the two superpowers. In its place, a new set of principles appears to have emerged. These take account of the existence of an allowed perimeter of superpower self-interest and self-defense that extends beyond the superpower borders to include the whole of its "region." Within that region its perceptions *are* fact and its self-interest *is* law. When the superpower determines that events in another state threaten its regional predominance or the orthodox homogeneity of the region, then it may put down the deviation, acting alone or with its regional retinue.

These new principles give the United States some advantages, but not surprisingly, the Soviets also felt free to take advantage of them in their own region and in their own way. This poses problems not only for small states in the superpower regions, but for world order. The U.N. Charter of 1945 may no longer be functional in 1970 in a world of covert warfare, nuclear peril, and Security Council deadlock. But the principles of unlimited unilateral discretion for superpowers, rules of practice that the USSR and the United States have apparently put in their place, create very serious new problems of their own.

The 1965 crisis concerning the Dominican Republic is an important instance of these new principles at work, as well as of the problems they raise. The United States made a unilateral finding of fact, on the basis of which it justified its unilateral use of force. As to these facts, there continues to be much to dispute. Many governments, not only those of the "socialist community" but even some of the most important and democratic of the American states—Chile, Mexico, Peru, Uruguay, Colombia, and Venezuela, among others—did not perceive the facts in the same way as did President Johnson, advised by Ambassador Bennett and Under Secretary Thomas C. Mann. Particularly controversial was the advice of Assistant Secretary Mann, who again played a key role, as he had in the Guatemalan affair. Specifically, most Latin-American states did not share our perception of the nature and extent of Communist danger in the revolution that ousted Santo Domingo's right-wing military dictatorship on April 24, 1965, and tried to restore the social democratic regime of former President Juan Bosch. It was by no means only foreign perceptions which differed from those of the United States government. So, too, did those of *The New York Times* correspondents.[1] Seyom Brown, social scientist for the Rand Corporation, wrote that the evidence of Communist or Castroite take-over of the revolution was "fragmentary" "uncertain" and "hyperbole"—a "numbers

---

1. For a comparative study of U.S. official reporting and the reporting of U.S. correspondents, especially to *The New York Times,* see Franck and Cherkis, "The Problem of Fact-Finding in International Disputes," 18 *Western Reserve Law Review,* Rev. 1483 (1967).

game." [2] This skepticism was echoed by Senator Fulbright among others in Congress.[3]

Even within the ranks of the U.S. government, there were the most serious doubts—about the nature of events in the Dominican Republic, about the wisdom of the intervention, and, particularly, about the verbal strategy employed to justify the unilateral use of force. Ambassador Adlai Stevenson's recent biographer, Richard Walton, reports, for example, that there is "absolutely no doubt that Stevenson was entirely against the American intervention . . . [and believed] that the Dominican intervention was a massive blunder." [4] Walton states categorically that "Stevenson . . . had to repeat endlessly statements he knew not to be true and justifications he believed indefensible. . . ." [5] He conjectures that Stevenson "might well have agreed with the pickets outside the U.S. Mission that any country, even a country in Latin America, had the right to choose any form of government it wanted, even Communism." [6]

Between the end of April and the middle of May, the United

2. Seyom Brown, *The Faces of Power,* New York: Columbia University Press, 1968, p. 357.
3. U.S. Senate, *Congressional Record,* Sept. 15, 1965, p. 23857. Different scholars also have written conflicting accounts of the Dominican events of 1965 and the rationale behind the U.S. intervention. Recently, for example, Jerome Slater, *Intervention and Negotiation: The United States and the Dominican Revolution,* New York: Harper & Row, 1970, disagrees in major aspects with Theodore Draper's account, "The Dominican Revolt," originally published in *Commentary,* 40, December 1965, pp. 33–68; also, Draper, "American Crisis: Vietnam, Cuba and the Dominican Republic," *Commentary,* 43, January 1967, pp. 27–48. For Draper's retort to Slater's more recently published book, see "The Dominican Intervention Reconsidered," *Political Science Quarterly,* LXXXVI, March 1971, pp. 1–36. Also see Jerome Slater, *OAS and U.S. Foreign Policy,* Columbus, Ohio: Ohio State University Press, 1967; Dan Kurzman, *Santo Domingo: Revolt of the Damned,* New York: G. P. Putnam, 1965; Jay Mallin, *Caribbean Crisis,* New York: Doubleday, 1965.
4. Richard Walton, *The Remnants of Power,* New York: Coward-McCann, 1968, p. 171.
5. *Ibid.,* p. 170.
6. *Ibid.,* p. 172.

States landed 21,500 Army, Marine, and Air Force personnel in the Dominican Republic.[7] The number eventually "peaked" at about 25,000,[8] and the last part of it was only withdrawn on September 21, 1966, almost seventeen months later.[9]

The verbal strategy of the United States in support of the troop landings was a masterpiece of muddle and ineffective planning. This was in part due to shortsightedness and in part to divisions within the government. The first justification advanced by President Johnson was that the troops were engaging in a humanitarian rescue of U.S. citizens caught in a tragic civil war.[10] But the United States position in this respect was not without its legal and political difficulties, even if it could have been shown that protection of U.S. citizens was the real basis for sending the troops. Similar reasons of protection had served to justify intervention in Latin America for a century [11] and more recently had been employed to validate U.S. troop landings in Lebanon and the Congo,[12] also in circumstances of civil war. There is, first of all, doubt about whether the humanitarian aspect of these operations was their principal motivation. But even if it was, there is doubt whether "humanitarian intervention" is a concept sanctioned by law. A study for the City Bar of New York notes that "some Latin Americans contend that intervention for the protection of lives and liberty of citizens abroad is outlawed by international

7. Note of May 22, Ambassador Ellsworth Bunker to William Sanders, Assistant Secretary General of the OAS. United States, Department of State, *Bulletin,* LII, 1965, p. 912.
8. Ruth Russell, *The United Nations and United States Security Policy,* Washington, D.C.: Brookings Institution, 1968, p. 181.
9. 11 OAS Chronicle, No. 2, October 1966, p. 2.
10. Statement by President Johnson, Apr. 28, 1965. United States, Department of State, *Bulletin,* LII, 1965, p. 738.
11. John Fagg, *Latin America, A General History,* New York: Macmillan, 1963; Donald Fox, "Doctrinal Development in the Americas: From Non-Intervention to Collective Support For Human Rights," 1 *New York University Journal of International Law and Politics,* 1968, p. 44.
12. Cf., United States, Department of State, *Bulletin,* L, 1964, pp. 838–46.

law, for a state is under no responsibility to grant greater protection to foreigners than to its own citizens. Accordingly, no state has a right to intervene in another state in favor of the life or liberty of its nationals." [13] The study, moreover, after examining the relevant legal documents, comes to the conclusion that in "view of the prohibition of the use or threat of force against the territorial integrity of a state set forth in the U.N. Charter, the strong language prohibiting intervention in the Charter of the OAS, and the prohibition against military occupation of a state or the use of other measures of force against a state, also in the Charter of the OAS, it can be said that armed intervention by a state on behalf of its nationals who have suffered injury and a denial of justice at the hands of another government in order to enforce reparation, to punish and prevent future repetition, i.e., to impose sanctions in the form of reprisals has been made illegal." [14] All other forms of armed intervention on behalf of nationals are likewise illegal, unless the threat to these nationals is to be regarded as an "armed attack" on the country from which the nationals came—an interpretation plainly not intended by either the U.N. Charter (Article 51) or the Pact of Bogota (Article 43). [15]

On April 30, President Johnson in a television broadcast asked the nation to understand that the troops had been sent "when, and only when, we were officially notified by police and

13. "The Dominican Republic Crisis 1965," *Background Paper and Proceedings of the ninth Hammarskjöld Forum*, A. J. Thomas, Jr., and A. van W. Thomas, Dobbs Ferry, New York: Oceana Press for the Association of the Bar of the City of New York, 1967, p. 10.
14. *Ibid.*, p. 13.
15. *Ibid.* For a corroborating thesis which demonstrates in detail that "Little support is found either factually or legally for the view that the United States was entitled to intervene to prevent a Communist takeover" and which also denies that the United States had the legal right to intervene in the Dominican Republic to rescue its own nationals, see Cynthia A. Walker, *International Legal Aspects of the Conflict in the Dominican Republic, 1965,* unpublished dissertation submitted to Girton College, Cambridge University, England, June 1970.

military officials of the Dominican Republic that they were no longer in a position to guarantee the safety of American and foreign nationals." He emphasized the argument that the intervention had been requested by the Dominican Republic itself. However, this time the phrase "and to preserve law and order" was added, as well as the suggestion, still vague, that "there are signs that people trained outside the Dominican Republic are seeking to gain control." [16] This was, however, a double-edged principle, since most foreign-trained personnel in the Dominican Republic were military officers trained in the United States.[17]

By May 1, the pattern of Washington's verbal strategy had begun to shift more noticeably. "Our goal in the Dominican Republic," the President declared to the OAS ". . . is that the people of that country must be permitted freely to choose the path of political democracy, social justice, and economic progress. . . . We intend to carry on the struggle against tyranny no matter in what ideology it cloaks itself. This is our mutual responsibility . . . and the common values which bind us together." [18] The "humanitarian" basis of the intervention had now yielded to another unilateral finding of "fact": the Communist conspiracy against the Dominican Republic and against the hemisphere. The United States was arrogating the right to use military force to ensure democratic process in a Latin-American nation which had been under U.S.- sponsored or -tolerated authoritarian regimes for much of its history.

This rhetoric, defending the use of force as a means to make the Dominican Republic safe for democracy, carried little more credibility than the invocation of the humanitarian-intervention principle. The next day, however, the specifically anti-Communist objective of the invasion was openly declared. On May 2, the

16. Statement by President Johnson, April 30, 1965. United States, Department of State, *Bulletin,* LII, 1965, p. 742.
17. Cf., Theodore Draper, *Abuse of Power,* New York: Viking Press, 1967, *passim.*
18. Statement by President Johnson, May 1, 1965. United States, Department of State, *Bulletin,* LII, 1965, pp. 743–44.

President, beginning simply enough, unveiled a momentous concept of compulsory hemispheric solidarity which did not lack credibility but which may be faulted, and most seriously, on strategic grounds. "I was sitting in my little office reviewing the world situation with Secretary Rusk, Secretary McNamara and Mr. McGeorge Bundy," Mr. Johnson explained. "Shortly after 3 o'clock I received a cable from our Ambassador, and he said that things were in danger; he had been informed the chief of police and governmental authorities could no longer protect us." [19] "Us" in this instance appeared to mean U.S. residents in the Dominican Republic. In fact, however, none had been in any way harmed up to this point. The President did not linger on this aspect. Instead, he went on to assert the unilateral right of the United States to intervene militarily in any sovereign state of the hemisphere if in the opinion of the United States that state were in danger of falling to the Communists. He drew no distinction between Communist accessions achieved by external invasion, internal coup, or democratic election; nor did he distinguish between Communist influence upon, infiltration into, or control of a revolutionary movement.

Why did the armed intervention begin with one justification and then shift in midstream to quite another? One account, by Stevenson's biographer, states that when President Johnson on April 28 showed advisers the draft of his initial statement, it contained two rationalizations for dispatching troops—the need to save American civilian lives and to safeguard against a Communist take-over. Walton maintains that it was Stevenson who objected to the second of these grounds and persuaded the President to omit it.[20] By May 2, more than half the U.S. civilians in Santo Domingo had already been evacuated. Meanwhile, however, the political situation had come to look more dangerous than ever. Obviously, the evacuation of U.S. civilians could not be used once again to justify a new expansion of the U.S. forces from a

19. Statement by President Johnson, May 2, 1965, *ibid.,* pp. 744–45.
20. Walton, *op. cit.,* pp. 168–69.

few thousand to over twenty thousand. There were simply not enough U.S. nationals to protect.

Then, too, the days between April 28 and May 2 had seen the unravelling of another part of the original "humanitarian" justification for the U.S. invasion. It had soon become apparent that the "invitation" by Dominican "authorities" had, in fact, come not from neutral officials responsible for law and order but from Colonel Benoit, the head of the junta faction.[21] The junta's reasons for calling in the United States were obviously not humanitarian but partisan. Colonel Benoit, in fact, was having some credibility problems of his own. On the one hand he maintained that he had made the request solely because he did not have enough troops to provide the protection urgently wanted by the diplomatic missions. Yet he also boasted, on the other hand, that he had not taken the city of Santo Domingo solely to prevent rebel casualties, although "he had enough forces to do so." [22] These claims are contradictory and unconvincing. A more credible estimate of the junta's military position before the large-scale U.S. landings was given by Mr. Leonard C. Meeker, the legal adviser in the Department of State, who candidly reported that during "the course of April 28 the anti-rebel forces lost their momentum after earlier progress. . . ." [23]

By May 2, there was a widespread belief that U.S. troops had been called in only after the junta had faltered in its efforts to capture Santo Domingo and put down the revolution.[24] The original humanitarian reasons for the intervention, although repeated by the President, no longer sufficed and were widely regarded as having been ill-advised. Now President Johnson de-

21. U.N. Doc. S/6364, 18 May 1965, p. 9, OAS Doc. 47. Letter by Col. Benoit to Ambassador Bennett, April 28, 1965, First Report of the Special Committee of the Tenth Meeting of Consultation of Ministers of Foreign Affairs of the American States.

22. *Ibid.,* p. 8.

23. Leonard C. Meeker, "The Dominican Situation in the Perspective of International Law." United States, Department of State, *Bulletin,* LIII, 1965, p. 61.

24. Thomas, *supra,* p. 6.

veloped a new verbal strategy in his broadcast: "Our goal, in keeping with the great principles of the Inter-American system, is to help prevent another Communist state in this hemisphere." [25] The President went on to enunciate the facts that determined his choice of the action necessary to preserve the national interest: "The revolutionary movement took a tragic turn. Communist leaders, many of them trained in Cuba, seeing a chance to increase disorder, to gain a foothold, joined the revolution. They took increasing control. And what began as a popular democratic revolution, committed to democracy and social justice, very shortly moved and was taken over and really seized and placed into the hands of a band of Communist conspirators." [26] In the haste and urgency of the moment, the President accidentally repeated this entire foregoing paragraph a second time some moments later in his speech.[27] He then spoke of the "international conspiracy from which United States servicemen have rescued the [Dominican] people . . ." [28] and went on to enunciate the Johnson Doctrine: the *"American nations cannot, must not, and will not permit the establishment of another Communist government in the Western Hemisphere."* [29] To justify this, he cited the precedents of OAS actions, including sanctions and the quarantine in the case of Cuba. The United States had made its findings of fact, had weighed their consequences, and had acted accordingly.

As has already been noted, neither the Cuban nor the Guatemalan precedent extends to an outright invasion by U.S. troops. This broader unilateral action had to be justified in terms of a broader new principle. The President indicated awareness that his action constituted the first overt, unilateral U.S. military intervention in a sovereign state since the establishment of the U.N. He showed concern that his objectives be achieved without ex-

25. Statement by President Johnson, May 2. United States, Department of State, *Bulletin,* LII, 1965, p. 747.
26. *Ibid.*
27. *Ibid.,* pp. 745–46.
28. *Ibid.*
29. *Ibid.,* p. 746. Italics ours.

cessive use of force—"we would like to do this without bloodshed or without large-scale fighting"—but he made it quite clear that in his opinion, the dispatching of U.S. troops to a sovereign country is justifiable if that state seems to be slipping its moorings in the non-Communist Inter-American community, and that U.S. troops would be used whether such intervention is requested by the threatened government or not. Mr. Johnson pointed out that the form of regime in a Latin-American state is not a matter solely for the people of that state. Thus, "we do know what kind of government we hope to see in the Dominican Republic. For that is carefully spelled out in the treaties and agreements which make up the fabric of the Inter-American system." [30] It is the obligation, and not merely the right of the community to take collective military action to maintain the integrity of that system when necessary. And until the community agrees to act, the United States has no choice but to act alone, for "it is our mutual responsibility to help the people of the Dominican Republic toward the day when they can freely choose the path of liberty and justice and progress. This is required of us by the agreements that we are party to and that we have signed. This is required of us by the values which bind us together." [31]

Culling Mr. Johnson's words at the United Nations, Adlai Stevenson fastened onto the simple statement, "the American nations will not permit the establishment of another Communist government in the Western hemisphere," [32] and thereby captured the essence and foreshadowed almost the exact text of the Brezhnev Doctrine.

Thereafter Secretary of State Rusk spelled out the surrogacy of the United States in enforcing the modalities of the Inter-American system in the Dominican Republic:

> What began in the Dominican Republic as a democratic revolution was taken over by Communist conspirators who

30. *Ibid.,* p. 747.
31. *Ibid.*
32. A. Stevenson, SCOR, S/PV. 1196th Mtg., 3 May 1965, p. 16.

had been trained for, and had carefully planned, that operation. Had they succeeded in establishing a government, the Communist seizure of power would, in all likelihood, have been irreversible, thus frustrating the declared principles of the OAS. We acted to preserve the freedom of choice of the Dominican people until the OAS could take charge and insure that the principles were carried out.[33]

Unfortunately the OAS had not at this time found, nor did it later find, that the facts were as the Secretary painted them, nor that the conclusions drawn from the facts were justified by hemispheric considerations of self-interest.

Among Mr. Johnson's advisers were several who would have preferred the emphasis of the President's words to have been not, as Mr. Stevenson paraphrased them, on a total prohibition against any hemispheric state "going Communist" by fair means or foul, but on a theory of collective self-defense against international aggression. But who could be said to have attacked the Dominican Republic? Helpfully, the State Department's legal adviser was able to produce an aggressor by means of another new doctrine— "participation in the Inter-American system, to be meaningful, must take into account the modern day reality that an attempt by a conspiratorial group inspired from the outside to seize control by force can be an assault upon the independence and integrity of a state." [34] An essentially similar term, "inspired by an outside power," is used again later in the legal adviser's memorandum [35] and in subsequent pronouncements.[36] Its significance lies in de-

33. Statement of Secretary of State Dean Rusk of May 8, 1965, in *The Dominican Crisis,* Department of State Pub. 7971, *Inter-American Series* 92 (1965); also, United States, Department of State, *Bulletin,* Vol. LII, 1965, p. 843.
34. Leonard C. Meeker, "Legal Basis for the United States Actions in the Dominican Republic," in Abram Chayes, Thomas Ehrlich and Andreas F. Lowenfeld, *International Legal Process: Materials for an Introductory Course,* Vol. II, New York: Little, Brown, 1969, p. 1182.
35. *Ibid.*
36. Cf., *ibid.,* and Meeker, *loc. cit.,* p. 62.

vising a conceptual strategy by which Dominicans can be deemed to be foreign aggressors *even in their own country* if they support efforts to establish a government which is "inspired" by a foreign regime or by an alien ideology. By virtue of this new definition of aggression, it becomes unnecessary to show an actual overt or covert armed attack by one state upon another before sending in U.S. troops for "collective self-defense." It is enough that elements seeking a change in government are "inspired" from abroad by training, money, teaching, and propaganda, or perhaps just by example. Once a Dominican becomes "inspired" by Cuba, Russia, or China, the argument suggests, he ceases to be a true Dominican and is transformed into a vicarious instrument of Cuban, Russian, or Chinese expansion. The political, revolutionary struggle in which he engages likewise ceases to be an internal one and becomes vicariously international, a case of aggression against which the superpower and the regional organization may respond in "self-defense" under Article 53 of the U.N. Charter and Article 3 of the Rio Pact.

All of these concepts were made to order for the Soviets and the Warsaw Pact in the summer of 1968. Within the principles the United States had enunciated, the Russian invaders were comfortably able to locate their own actions. If "inspiration" by foreign ideology, propaganda or influence is sufficient to transform Dominicans into vicarious Cubans, it is equally able to transform democratizing Czechoslovaks into vicarious American imperialists or "revanchist" West Germans, and having been so transformed, they too become "foreign" aggressors in their own countries, justifying the use of force by the regional superpower and a concert of regional states in "collective self-defense" of the Czechoslovak people and "the socialist community."

But the Johnson Doctrine did not merely justify U.S. unilateral intervention or OAS multilateral action on the basis of collective self-defense against an act of aggression. It goes even further in its assertion of principle, claiming the right of the United States to intervene simply and directly whenever necessary to prevent "the establishment of another Communist government in the Western Hemisphere," whether it is seeking power by internal or external means. Also, according to the Johnson Doctrine, it is the U.S. leaders who in any instance will determine whether such a Communist take-over is occurring. Even the indigenous non-Communist forces apparently cannot be trusted to know when they are being victimized. Juan Bosch was the case in point. The first president-designate of the Dominican revolution maintained, throughout, that the "truth is that the constitutional forces are not under communist influence. They are in control of the situation. By themselves, they are stronger, militarily, than the Wessin forces." [37] This view was largely upheld by *The New York Times* dispatches.[38] And Colonel Caamano, the leader of the revolutionary [constitutional] forces, stated categorically that "We have no communist problem." [39] Both these Dominican leaders were acknowledged by the U.S. government to be non-Communists. Their efforts to convince an unheeding United States government that they were well able to judge and meet the danger of infiltration into their reform movement sounds pathetically like Mr. Dubcek's desperate last-minute efforts to do the same in relation to the Warsaw Pact nations. The pleas of Bosch and Caamano foreshadowed Foreign Minister Hajek's pathetic effort at the U.N. Security Council after the invasion of his country to convince his unwelcome protectors that "nothing could justify the apprehensions and doubts about an alleged danger of counter-revolution in the Czechoslovak Socialist Republic. The Government had the situation firmly in hand. . . ." [40]

But a fact, both small states learned, is an opinion held by a

37. Quoted by F. A. Tabio, SCOR, S/PV. 1198th Mtg., 4 May 1965, p. 21.
38. Tad Szulc, *The New York Times,* May 2–5, 1965, p. 1, Editorial, *The New York Times,* May 3, 1965, p. 32, May 4, 1965, p. 42; P. Kihss, *The New York Times,* May 4, 1965, p. 14.
39. Tabio, *supra,* n. 37.
40. J. Hajek, 23 U.N. SCOR S/PV.1445, 1445th Mtg., 24 August 1968, p. 101.

superpower. The implication of the Johnson and Brezhnev doctrines is that the decision as to what constitutes a sufficient danger of subversion in a small power to warrant great-power intervention is too important a matter to be decided by the small state. Only Ambassador Stevenson among leading officials gave public expression to a modicum of confidence in the ability of the Dominican revolutionary leaders to fend for themselves. "The great majority of those who joined in this insurgent cause in the Dominican Republic are not Communists," he said in the Security Council. But then he too, as the representative of the mighty power which had already decided the matter, turned his attention to the "small group of well-known Communists" who "with their usual tactics" were known to have "attempted to seize control of the revolution." [41] The purity and orthodoxy of non-Communist movements in Latin America and of Communist ones in Eastern Europe are, it seems, to be guaranteed by the dominant superpower in each region.

This choice of U.S. verbal strategy was of immense importance. One wonders whether those who spoke the words listened to them with sufficient care for their middle- and long-term implications—both for the future of systemic U.S.-Latin-American relations and for the reciprocal use the Soviets would make of the same doctrine in Moscow's relations with Eastern Europe. Senator Fulbright, who did listen in this way, heard the Johnson Doctrine with alarm, not so much on account of what had already been done under its aegis as for what it portended:

> Intervention on the basis of Communist participation as distinguished from control of the Dominican revolution was a mistake in my opinion which also reflects a grievous misreading of the temper of contemporary Latin American politics. Communists are present in all Latin American countries, and they are going to inject themselves into almost any Latin American revolution and try to seize control of it. If any group or any movement with which the Com-

41.   A. Stevenson, SCOR, S/PV. 1196th Mtg., 3 May 1965, p. 13.

munists associate themselves is going to be automatically condemned in the eyes of the United States, then we have indeed given up all hope of guiding or influencing even to a marginal degree the revolutionary movements and the demands for social change which are sweeping Latin America. Worse, if that is our view, then we have made ourselves the prisoners of the Latin American oligarchs who are engaged in a vain attempt to preserve the status quo—reactionaries who habitually use the term "Communist" very loosely, in part out of emotional predilection and in part in a calculated effort to scare the United States into supporting their selfish and discredited aims.[42]

Liberal forces in the American states were not slow to grasp the dangers of the Johnson Doctrine. Its promise to prevent another Cuba was no doubt welcome enough. But the undertaking to nip any Communist bud anywhere, anytime, at the sole determination and discretion of the United States government was not an acceptable formula for achieving continental security. When a myopic giant sets out to rid his house of flies, no winged creature sleeps soundly. The more democratic of the American nations naturally recoiled at the tutelage concept. But even the others feared that a practice of intervention against Communism could in the wrong hands become a justification for intervening on the side of democracy against rightist dictators. *L'appétit vient en mangeant.*

Inter-American displeasure with the invasion of the Dominican Republic, particularly with U.S. justifications for its actions, found expression in various ways. The Latin-American states frustrated the achievement of certain U.S. objectives, such as keeping the U.N. out, establishing a genuine multilateral regional peace-force, and getting the regional organization to adopt and thus legitimate the principles on which the United States had acted. The effect of the Johnson Doctrine was to launch principles or reinforce and extend ones previously launched, which the

42. United States Senate, Congressional Record, Senator Fulbright, September 15, 1965, p. 23858.

Soviet Union was only too happy to apply within its own regional ghetto. But it gained us nothing in return, merely adding to the hostility with which the Dominican invasion was greeted by most Latin American states. The principles of the Johnson Doctrine certainly did not make the U.S. action more palatable to other Latin Americans. It did not unite the people of the United States behind the President. It did not seem to have the effect of subsequently frightening the more independent-minded states like Peru, Bolivia, or Chile into strict orthodoxy or conformity. In all, it seems to have been a bad bargain, in effect sanctioning Russia's invasion of Czechoslovakia while asserting for the United States, throughout Latin America, sweeping rights which we possibly never meant to exercise, but the assertion of which cost us heavily in the goodwill of our neighbors.

At the United Nations the representative of Uruguay took the unprecedented step not only of criticizing the United States but of introducing a resolution that ran counter to stated U.S. interests.[43] Ambassador Velazquez charged on May 4 that a "grave armed situation . . . had arisen owing to the landing of forces of an American State" and that his country "repudiated the acts of intervention carried out in contravention of articles 15 and 17 of the OAS charter." [44] He reminded the U.S. with passionate eloquence that the OAS charter "prohibits in the most explicit and categorical manner any form of intervention, direct or indirect, by one State or by a group of States, for any reason whatever—let me repeat, for any reason whatever—in the internal or external affairs of any other contracting State" and "that the territory of an American State is inviolable; it may not be the object, even temporarily, of military occupation or of other measures of force taken by another State, directly or indirectly, on any grounds whatever—I repeat, on any grounds whatever." The ambassador also emphasized that "this Johnson Doctrine . . . cannot be re-

43. A. Stevenson, SCOR, 1204th Mtg., 11 May 1965, pp. 16–17. Uruguay's Draft Resolution is U.N. Doc. S/6346, 21 May 1965.
44. C. Velazquez, SCOR, 1198th Mtg., 4 May 1965, p. 3.

garded as a legal doctrine, for the idea it embodies—that while revolutions are prima facie the internal affairs of countries and for them alone to deal with, they cease to be so and become matters calling for hemispheric action when their object is to establish a communist dictatorship—seems to go beyond the body of norms existing in the Inter-American system and constitutes, in its spirit and letter, a notion which my delegation cannot regard as consistent with the principle of self-determination of peoples." [45] As for the idea that earlier decisions and declarations by the OAS—particularly that of Punta del Este—could serve as a precedent for such intervention, the ambassador, representing the country which had been host to the eighth meeting of consultation, declared:

> The only conclusion to be drawn from resolution VI of the Punta del Este Meeting of Consultation was that of the exclusion from the organs of the Inter-American system of the Cuban Government or any other government associated with the same ideological or political system. No single word in this resolution—and let me say in passing that this is the most extreme decision ever adopted in the Inter-American system on a matter of general principle—allows the resolution to be regarded as authorizing the type of action which has been carried out or which might be carried out in future in any of our countries.

He further stated:

> Neither can my delegation agree that the doctrine expounded by President Johnson and reiterated here by the representative of his Government may be considered at this juncture to be a common doctrine of the American Republics. This doctrine—like its remote predecessor, the Monroe Doctrine, and like the first corollaries to that doctrine, the Olney corollary and the Roosevelt corollary—is a . . . purely unilateral policy formulated on its own responsibility by the Government of the United States.[46]

45. *Ibid.*, pp. 4–5.
46. *Ibid.*, pp. 5–6.

With even its own Latin-American alliance so shaky, Washington was understandably reluctant to usher a U.N. presence into the situation. Indeed, the U.S. representative struggled mightily to keep the matter "in the family." Again, as in the Guatemalan case, a positive U.N. role was deplored as counter-productive and intrusive. We reinforced our previous contention that disputes within our region were no one else's concern. The Uruguayan resolution, in the words of Ambassador Stevenson, sought "to interpose the Security Council into the situation. . . ." Such interposition, the U.S. argued, "would tend to complicate the activities of the Organization of American States by encouraging concurrent and independent considerations and activities by this Council." [47] Uruguay, on the other hand, emphasized that the U.N. had every right to inquire into this situation, one which might threaten the peace, "even if the dispute is at the time under consideration by a regional body." [48] So isolated was the United States, that it could not prevail in the argument—firmly adhered to in the Guatemalan case—that the matter was one that concerned only the OAS and was outside the U.N.'s jurisdiction. Accordingly, the U.S. representative softened the position, stating that his government "welcomes the discussion," [49] but adding that "it would be constructive and in keeping with the precedents established by this Council to permit the regional organization to continue to deal with this regional problem." [50] Ruth Russell aptly paraphrased the outcome: "Lacking strong Latin-American support, the United States therefore accepted a resolution that described the Security Council as 'deeply concerned at the grave events in the Dominican Republic,' called for a strict cease-fire, and 'invited' the Secretary-General to send a representative to 'report' on the 'present situation' to the Council." [51]

47. A. Stevenson, SCOR, 1204th Mtg., 11 May 1965, p. 17.
48. C. Velazquez, *supra*, p. 6.
49. A. Stevenson, *supra*, n. 47.
50. *Ibid.*, p. 18.
51. Russell, *op. cit.*, n. 8, p. 183. The resolution is U.N. Doc. S/Res. 203, May 14, 1965.

U.S. policies had even rougher passage behind the closed doors of Inter-American negotiating meetings. Here U.S. policies, both its action and its principles, ran into opposition from the "family" at every turn. There was the humiliating fiasco of the so-called OAS force. Although an Inter-American force was voted into existence by the OAS on May 6, by May 19 the 21,500 U.S. troops had only been augmented by offers of 21 policemen from Costa Rica, 250 Honduran and 166 Nicaraguan soldiers, and 3 officers from El Salvador.[52] By June 3, Brazil had committed 1,114 troops and a chaplain, and Paraguay 183 soldiers.[53] This could scarcely be interpreted as overwhelmingly encouraging, not even by Secretary Rusk, who on June 2 allowed that "it is obvious to everyone there is a certain imbalance in the forces of the Inter-American Force at the present time."[54] It was particularly embarrassing that only the military dictatorships sent troops, and not many at that. The effort of an OAS force is particularly pathetic when compared with the regimented marshaling of Warsaw Pact forces to occupy Czechoslovakia. It showed that even when the United States sets out to use force to compel a recalcitrant member of its sphere of influence to toe the line, it cannot quite bring itself to exert the additional force necessary to make the other states of the sphere participate in the dirty work. The Russians have no such scruples. This at least raises the question whether an international arrangement that gives each superpower an unlimited right to brutalize its satellites will not inevitably favor the superpower most prepared to use this right to the utmost. When Romans compete with Vandals they ought not to agree to do it on Vandal terms.

The efforts by the U.S. to develop principles and practices

52. Second Report of the Special Committee of the Tenth Meeting of Consultation of Ministers of Foreign Affairs, Doc. 81, U.N. Doc. S/6370, 19 May 1965, p. 12; hereafter referred to as *Second Report*.
53. 1 OAS Chronicle, No. 1, August 1965, p. 5.
54. Statement by Secretary Rusk, OAS to Help Restore Democratic Order in Dominican Republic. United States, Department of State, *Bulletin*, LII, 1965, p. 1017.

that would transform the U.S. invasion into an OAS operation were costly not only to the extent that it was resisted but also to the extent that it was successful in effecting the transformation. Professor Jerome Slater correctly notes that "the legitimizing capacity of the OAS is sharply reduced to the extent that the Organization is believed to be dominated by the United States . . . and it is probable that this perception is growing. . . ." [55] When we tried to legitimize our invasion by transforming it into a regional peacekeeping operation, we lost both ways, we were largely unable to compel the regional states to go along with the gambit, and those who did go along only confirmed the discrediting popular view of the OAS as a tool of U.S. imperialism.

From the beginning, all efforts to have the Latin-American states fall in line with the principles governing the U.S. initiative ran into difficulty. Washington had pressed the meeting of consultation to take a position similar to its own and even to adopt the U.S. intervention as the OAS had previously ratified the Cuban quarantine. Not only would this have assembled the Latin-American states behind the U.S. political action, but it would, in the opinion of the leading U.S. legal authorities, have provided the most legitimate conceptual basis for the military intervention, if not in terms of the U.N. Charter then at least in OAS jurisprudence. In the opinion of Professor C. G. Fenwick, "the wide competence of the Organ of Consultation under Article 8 of the Rio Treaty would easily have justified the occupation of the island by an 'Inter-American Armed Force' in spite of the strong terms of Article 17 of the [OAS] Charter." [56] Professor Thomas in his study similarly notes that the OAS could have legitimized the United States and its own subsequent actions by proceeding with collective self-defense against a Communist attack under Article 3

55. J. Slater, "The Limits of Legitimization in International Organizations: The Organization of American States and the Dominican Crisis," 23 *International Organization,* 1 (Winter 1969), p. 53.
56. Fenwick, "The Dominican Republic: Intervention on Collective Self-Defense," 60 *American Journal of International Law* (1966), p. 64 at p. 66.

of the Rio Treaty or by finding a threat short of an actual attack under Article 6.[57] The more significant, therefore, is the failure of the regional organization to bestow its imprimatur. The United States was simply unable to obtain the two-thirds majority necessary for such action in the meeting of consultation.[58] So contrary was the response of the Latin-American governments, that it took an entire week—under direct political pressure—to marshal the two-thirds majority necessary even to establish the Inter-American force.[59] At that, Chile, Mexico, Uruguay, Peru, and Ecuador opposed the resolution, with Venezuela abstaining.[60] The hairbreadth majority was made possible only by recognizing "the vote of the Dominican representative of a presumably non-existent government. . . ." [61]

Where the OAS did participate in the operation, it did little to endorse the principles set out by Washington. Buried just beneath the surface of OAS reports on conditions in the Dominican Republic during the occupation, there can be found a large number of critical references to "the lesions suffered by the principle of non-intervention." [62] Along similar lines, on January 19, 1966, Ambassador de Lavalle of Peru requested the convocation of a special meeting of the Council of the OAS "to formulate a denunciation on the violation of the principle of non-intervention. . . ." [63] The special committee established on May 1, 1965, by the tenth meeting of consultation of the OAS "to carry out an investigation of all aspects of the situation in the Dominican Republic that led to the convocation of this meeting" [64] notably failed to substantiate the U.S. view expressed by Under Secretary Thomas Mann that "the paramilitary forces under the control of

57. Thomas and Thomas, *supra*, n. 13, pp. 38–52.
58. Fenwick, *supra*, n. 56, p. 66.
59. Russell, *supra*, n. 8, p. 181.
60. United States, Department of State, *Bulletin*, LII, 1965, p. 862; also Russell, *supra*, n. 8, p. 181.
61. Russell, *supra*, n. 8, p. 181.
62. *Second Report, supra*, n. 52, p. 12.
63. 1 OAS Chronicle, No. 5, April 1966, p. 2.
64. 1 OAS Chronicle, No. 1, August 1965, p. 2.

known Communists exceeded in military strength the forces controlled by the non-Communist elements within the rebel movement" and that "these non-Communist elements were working hand in glove with the Communists." [65] Indeed, the only shred of evidence to support this view is a brief and inconclusive mention by the Committee of an encounter with a Frenchman called Rivière. Even at that, Rivière is not named as a Communist.[66] If the rebel forces were laced with Reds, the Committee wholly failed to see them.

During its first plenary session, the OAS meeting of consultation established a special committee composed of representatives of Argentina, Brazil, Colombia, Guatemala, and Panama to go to the Dominican Republic "to offer its good offices to the Dominican armed groups and political groups and to diplomatic representatives for the purpose of obtaining urgently: i. A cease-fire; and ii. The orderly evacuation of persons who have taken asylum in diplomatic missions and of all foreign citizens who desire to leave the Dominican Republic. . . ." [67] The resolution also calls on the special committee to investigate the current situation, but utters no word of judgment or condemnation against any faction, nor does it endorse the U.S. initiative in dispatching troops. In the controversial debate preceding the narrow passage of the resolution of May 6 calling for an Inter-American Force, Ambassador Bunker, the U.S. representative, found himself constantly on the defensive, with the support of only a few, primarily right-wing, governments. Even nations that voted for the resolution were highly critical of U.S. conduct, particularly of its verbal behavior. It is also instructive that Ambassador Bunker's defenses of U.S. policy now scrupulously avoided restating anything resembling the Johnson Doctrine. He made only a very few passing references to communism and foreign intervention, but heavily

65. Address by the Hon. Thomas C. Mann, Under Secretary of State for Economic Affairs, Department of State Press Release 241, October 12, 1965, pp. 9–10.
66. *First Report, supra,* n. 81, p. 7.
67. 1 OAS Chronicle, August 1965, p. 2.

emphasized the humanitarian aspect of the U.S. landings, an action intended to end bloodshed and permit the Dominican people to rebuild their shattered society and democratic instruments of self-determination.[68] It was solely this rationale that was incorporated in the OAS resolution calling for the establishment of the Inter-American force. Moreover, the humanitarian situation to which the resolution refers is not identical to the one described by President Johnson. The President had sought to justify the intervention on the ground that the lives of U.S. citizens were in danger. The OAS was concerned with danger to the lives of Dominicans. The purpose both of the force and of the continuing Meeting of Consultation was stated to be one and one alone:

> This force will have as its sole purpose, in a spirit of democratic impartiality, that of co-operating in the restoration of normal conditions in the Dominican Republic, in maintaining the security of its inhabitants and the inviolability of human rights, and in the establishment of an atmosphere of peace and conciliation that will permit the functioning of democratic institutions.[69]

The OAS would "facilitate the prompt restoration of democratic order in the Dominican Republic." [70]

Reporting on the work of a team of U.S. officials headed by McGeorge Bundy and dispatched to the Dominican Republic on May 14 by President Johnson, Ambassador Bunker noted that they had gone

> to lend maximum assistance to the OAS and to the people and leaders of the Dominican Republic: to help bring an

68. Ambassador Bunker, statements of May 1–14 to the Tenth Meeting of Consultation of the Ministers of Foreign Affairs of the OAS. OAS Foreign Ministers Provide for Establishment of Inter-American Force in Dominican Republic. United States, Department of State, *Bulletin,* LII, 1965, pp. 854–68.
69. OAS Resolution of May 6, 1965, Establishing Inter-American Force, *ibid.,* p. 863.
70. See, *ibid.,* pp. 862–63.

end to the fighting and bloodshed; to aid in the establishment of a broadly representative government based on
democratic, constitutional principles; [and] to help eliminate
the threat of present or future subversion of the Government of the Dominican Republic by Communist or other
extremist elements who might attempt to establish a regime
incompatible with the oft-declared principles of the inter-
American system.[71]

The third of these three objectives of U.S. intervention was not
then nor subsequently ever endorsed by the OAS. As long as
United States verbal strategy focused on the principle of humanitarian intervention to contain a prolonged, inconclusive, and bloody
civil war, a number, perhaps even a numerical majority of Latin-
American states, were willing under pressure to extend a grudging
endorsement to that principle. But various U.S. leaders from the
President down continued to assert a different principle—the right
of the superpower to intervene with force in any state within the
region to suppress what it perceived to be a Communist threat.
This doctrine of limited sovereignty was the broadest net we could
possibly have thrown over our actions; it was the most costly of
all possible rationalizations for U.S. conduct. As Seyom Brown
has said, the U.S. role in the Dominican Republic could be seen
as necessary or as a mistake made in haste, but what galled and
cost most "were the Administration's attempts to convert the rationalizations for its hasty action into a philosophy of contemporary statecraft." [72] The verbal strategy of the Johnson Administration put the United States on the line, endorsing a doctrine of
unlimited superpower supremacy in its region. This doctrine was
one we had great difficulty and little success in getting endorsed
by the Latin-American states. On the contrary, the principle

71. Ambassador Bunker, statement of May 18 to the Tenth Meeting
of Consultation of the Ministers of Foreign Affairs of the OAS.
OAS Secretary General to Represent Meeting of Consultation in
Dominican Republic. Brazilian to Command Inter-American Force.
Ibid., p. 909.
72. Brown, *op. cit.,* p. 359.

seemed primarily to alienate these states from our purposes in the Dominican Republic. But the same principles we here embraced proved very convenient to Soviet strategists in 1968. And they had far less difficulty in making the doctrine effective among the more docile nations of the Warsaw Pact. In other words, our verbal strategy in the Dominican case gained us little by way of support for that particular operation, but helped to establish a principle which lowered the cost when Russia and its allies invaded Czechoslovakia.

6

The Dominican Crisis
and the Czech Crisis:
The Echo Phenomenon

Despite the many similarities in verbal behavior, there are two important respects in which the case of the Dominican Republic can be said to fall short of being an exact precedent for the invasion of Czechoslovakia. In the first place, the Dominican intervention did terminate fairly quickly in what appears to have been democratic elections,[1] while the Soviet squeeze of Czechoslovakia goes on and on. And, secondly, while the Dominican Republic, like Cuba and Hungary, was easily accessible to the invading superpower's forces but relatively inaccessible to the rival superpower, Czechoslovakia, logistically, was almost equally accessible to both. Thus the invader's risk-taking in the instance of the Czechoslovak invasion seems at first glance much greater than in the other crises.

The Soviet Union did what it could to diminish this risk; it

1. On Sept. 3, 1965, Dr. Garcia Godoy assumed the provisional presidency; 1 OAS Chronicle No. 2, October 1965, p. 1. On June 1, 1966, presidential elections were held; II OAS Chronicle No. 1, August 1966, p. 2; and on September 21, 1966 the last contingents of the Inter-American Force departed; II OAS Chronicle No. 2, October 1966, p. 2.

attempted to reassure the West that the Warsaw Pact troops were not embarking on a new wave of conquest but merely engaging in a little family counseling, much as had the United States in Guatemala, Cuba, and the Dominican Republic. To make the "peaceful" nature of the Soviet invasion of Czechoslovakia absolutely credible and intelligible to the United States, the Soviets had the help of the words, concepts, and principles of prior U.S. foreign policy pronouncements.

Whatever the differences in actual conduct, the parallels between the verbal behavior of the Soviet Union and the United States in the Dominican and Czechoslovak crises are as symmetrical as a classical ballet, with the two powers in the second movement neatly changing roles and dancing each other's steps.

This study has so far focused on the verbal strategy of the United States. In order to appreciate the extraordinary reversal of roles which occurred in the Czechoslovak crisis, it is necessary to revert briefly to the verbal behavior of the Soviet Union during the Dominican episode. Here Russia advanced self-justifying propositions almost diametrically opposite those it was later to assert during its Czechoslovak invasion but uncannily similar to those propounded by the United States in August, 1968. But the principles we were championing during the Czechoslovak crisis were in turn the same as those advanced by the Russians during the Dominican invasion—promises we had rejected at the time. And the propositions advanced by the United States during the Dominican crisis closely paralleled those of the Soviets during the Czechoslovak invasion. This interchangeability is what we refer to as "the echo phenomenon."

The Soviet pronouncements during the take-over of the Dominican Republic were strident but clear. Ambassador Fedorenko enunciated principles worthy of greater sincerity:

> There can be no justification for the invasion of the territory of a sovereign State by United States armed forces.
>
> Such an act of undisguised arbitrariness is a cynical violation of the elementary norms of international law and of

the United Nations Charter, which forbids the threat or use of force against the territorial integrity or political independence of any State in international relations.[2]

Ambassador Fedorenko accused the United States of covering up "its armed intervention" by "trying to retreat behind the screen of the Organization of American States, which it long ago placed in the service of its imperialist designs."[3] What the United States had tried to justify as humanitarian intervention was no more than "brazen armed intervention" designed to "suppress the struggle of . . . patriotic forces"—a "criminal action by the forces of colonialism and imperialism. . . ."[4] The United States

> tries again and again to conduct itself in Latin America— and not only in that area—as if it was in its own private domain [and] gives itself the "right" to undertake punitive military action against national liberation movements. It decides when and where it should act as judge and assume the shameful role of executioner, using as cover the dirty and thoroughly dishonest pretext of the "need to restore law and order" in other countries, as if it were a question of Alabama or Mississippi.[5]

As for the real aims of the United States, the Soviets thought them perfectly apparent: "to impose on the Dominican people, from outside, a régime hateful to them; to suppress patriotic forces in the country fighting for its independence; and to ensure maximum profits for United States monopolies."[6]

Yet, in August 1968, the invasion of Czechoslovakia was justified by Moscow as regional self-defense against alien-influenced incursion, as a right and duty established by the Warsaw

2. Letter dated 1 May 1965 from the Permanent Representative of the Union of Soviet Socialist Republics addressed to the President of the Security Council Enclosing a Statement of Tass; U.N. Doc. S/6316, 20 U.N. SCOR Supp. May–June 1965, p. 46.
3. *Ibid.,* p. 45.
4. N. T. Fedorenko, Security Council, 1196th Mtg., 3 May 1965, p. 4.
5. *Ibid.,* pp. 5–6.
6. *Ibid.,* p. 7.

Pact, and as a humanitarian rescue operation. But back in 1965, when the shoe was on the other foot, the Soviets had experienced no difficulty seeing through the verbiage about self-defense, legality and humanitarianism:

> . . . armed interference by the United States in the domestic affairs of the Dominican Republic constitutes military aggression, an openly arbitrary act, and a violation both of the elementary rules of international law and of the United Nations Charter. The attempts of the United States Government to assume the role of ruler of the destinies of peoples, to dictate its will to them and to deal summarily with national liberation movements cannot be tolerated.[7]

The Soviets were not going to be put off substantive issues by deceptive formalism. They could see that the

> situation is, of course, not at all as the United States tries to present it. We should remember the truth, enshrined in the United Nations Charter but long forgotten by the United States, that it is for the peoples of all countries to choose whatever system they please and that no one has the right to interfere in their domestic affairs.[8]

In these circumstances

> the claim by the United States representative that the question of United States intervention in the Dominican Republic should be referred to the Organization of American States for consideration looks like a pitiful and cowardly attempt on the part of the United States to escape responsibility.[9]

During the Dominican debate in the Security Council, the Soviet representative pointed dramatically to the U.N. Charter's limitations on the use of force in self-defense and by regional organizations. Both self-defense and regional dispute settlement, he

7. *Ibid.,* p. 9.
8. *Ibid.,* p. 43.
9. *Ibid.*

knew, could become pretexts for ruthless aggression. For this reason the charter closely defines and limits both rights. The United States had ignored these limitations:

> Did the United States have . . . authorization from the Security Council? Perhaps Mr. Stevenson would be good enough to answer this question.

> By what right, under what charter, on what basis did the invasion by United States troops take place?

> It is no mere chance that my United States colleague has preferred to remain silent on this key question. For what the United States is doing is using armed force in violation of the United Nations Charter, in violation even of the Charter of the Organization of American States.[10]

This, of course, was exactly what the Soviets and their allies did in August 1968.

The Kremlin even had a theory about U.S. motivations which exactly previews the U.S. view of Soviet motives in 1968.

> Because of their abject poverty in the sphere of ideology, *Weltanschauung,* morality and philosophy, they have nothing with which to counter advanced ideas and a progressive outlook; in their rage and frenzy, they rush to take up arms and try by brute force to put down any people which is trying to achieve independence.[11]

This presents serious dangers, the Soviets argued, for the world no longer can have any certitudes about the future so long as the United States "in its hysteria" asserts "that democracy can be preserved only at the point of its soldiers' bayonets which are dripping with the blood of patriots" and its policies are set by "murderous," "irrational," "reckless," "imperialists" who are "obsessed with plots and see ghosts, mysteries and conspiracies" in their "frenzied anti-communist hysteria. . . ." [12] Again, this was

10.   *Ibid.,* p. 44.
11.   N. T. Fedorenko, Security Council, 1204th Mtg., 11 May 1965, p. 12.
12.   *Ibid.,* p. 13.

almost exactly the reaction in Western capitals to the events of August 1968. United States leaders solemnly concluded that their Soviet counterparts had revealed themselves as irrational, hysterical men who might stop at nothing.[13] The Senate Subcommittee on National Security emphasized the "similarities between Moscow's forcible methods and Nazi tactics and deeds. . . ." [14] without, however, seeing any similarities to those of the U.S. government.

In 1965 Soviet spokesmen landed hard on the assertion by President Johnson that "the right to decide the fate of [the Dominican Republic] rests only 'partly with the people of that country and partly with their neighbours.' " Such a concept of limited sovereignty the Russians found outrageous:

> It is hardly necessary to prove in any detail that such statements are incompatible with the obligations assumed by the United States under the Charter of the United Nations, which prohibits any interference in the internal affairs of other countries.[15]

Mr. Fedorenko was unequivocal on this point:

> In all this shameless farce only one thing is forgotten: the question of internal organization and régime is purely an internal affair of the Dominican people themselves and they alone—entirely alone—have the right to decide it without any pressure or interference from outside.[16]

Merciful history removed both Ambassadors Stevenson and Fedorenko from the United Nations scene before they were compelled by their governments' policies to don each other's clothes

13. *Czechoslovakia and the Brezhnev Doctrine,* Subcommittee on National Security and International Operations of the Committee on Government Operations, United States Senate, Washington, D.C.: U.S. Government Printing Office, 1969, p. 9.
14. *Ibid.*, p. 8.
15. N. T. Fedorenko, Security Council, 1220th Mtg., 3 June 1965, p. 14.
16. *Ibid.*, p. 13.

and speak each other's lines. If, however, it is striking that so many of the things Ambassador Fedorenko said at the time of the Dominican crisis were diametrically the opposite of what his successor, Mr. Malik, asserted during the Czechoslovak invasion, it is incomparably more significant for us that the justifications used by Mr. Malik in 1968 were virtually identical to the principles propounded by President Johnson, Ambassador Stevenson, Secretary Rusk, Ambassador Bunker, Legal Adviser Meeker and other key U.S. spokesmen at the time of the Dominican landings. Thus while the comparison of the contrast between Soviet verbal behavior in 1965 and 1968 merely reveals diplomatic hypocrisy, a comparison of the similarities between U.S. verbal strategy in 1965 and Soviet verbal strategy in 1968 raises more profound questions and concerns.

These questions do not deal with legal abstractions or with airy morality. The purpose of verbal strategy in international relations is to secure the national interest. And the consequence of imprudent verbal strategy is loss. For example, does the similarity in verbal behavior between the leaders and spokesmen for the two superpowers prove that both are equally hypocrites—and is such an equation in the popular mind of the world more to the disadvantage of the Soviets or of the United States? Does the elaborate quadrille, the echo phenomenon, prove the meaninglessness of all international legal reasoning, all professions of principled conduct, and is the growing worldwide impression to this effect a matter of equal indifference to the Soviet Union and the United States? Still more important—is the similarity of verbal behavior tantamount to an implied contract between the two superpowers to establish regional ghettos, an agreement upon which both may rely? And is such a contract equally to the benefit of both countries? Or do both nations really fail to see the similarity, so that each comprehends no relation between the rights it asserts within its own community and the assertion of parallel rights by the other superpower? If the answer to this last question is in the affirmative, there may be a wide gulf between what each side of the cold war believes it has a right to expect of the other, a predictability gap that could hinder systemic crisis management to the common disadvantage of both superpowers in particular and mankind in general.

The parallelism between Soviet verbal strategy in August 1968 and that of the United States in May–June 1965 is almost grimly poetic and extends even to subsidiary avowals and principles. Did the United States allege that it had been invited into the Dominican Republic? Russia and its allies similarly

> entered the territory of the Czechoslovak Socialist Republic on the basis of the request of the Government of that State, which applied to the allied Governments for assistance, including assistance with armed forces, in view of the threats created by the external and internal reaction to the socialist system and to the statehood established by the Constitution of Czechoslovakia.[17]

Exactly as with the U.S. cover story, so the account of this invitation by the Warsaw Pact nations wavered, changed, fell apart, and was eventually abandoned in favor of other explanations and justifications.[18] For a short time it was stated that the invitation, if not exactly issuing from the government of Czechoslovakia, did, at least, come from the faction most loyal to the norms of the Communist family—"leading party leaders and statesmen of Czechoslovakia loyal to the cause of socialism."[19] But even that much proved to be without foundation.

Did the United States justify its entry into the Dominican Republic on the ground that the international enemy conspiracy would otherwise have subverted the nation from its adherence to the regional norms? Russia, too, acted only after coming into

17. J. Malik, Security Council, 21 August 1968, S/PV.1441, p. 2.
18. Cf., Ambassador Ball's exposure of the discrepancies in the cover story as put out by the various Warsaw Pact governments. Security Council, 21 August 1968, S/PV.1441, pp. 17–21, and the Czech denial of an official invitation to the invaders, *ibid.*
19. J. Malik, Security Council, 24 August 1968, S/PV.1445, p. 117.

possession of "irrefutable data concerning ties between the internal reaction in Czechoslovakia and the outside world, with those who are interested in pulling Czechoslovakia out of the Socialist community of States." [20] The difficulties in Czechoslovakia are "certainly not fortuitous, since support for the international forces of reaction in the whole world in the fight against socialism and popular democracy has for a long time been one of the main elements in the policy of the ruling circles of the United States." [21] In other words, the United States opposes Soviet communist hegemony; certain elements in Czechoslovakia oppose Soviet communist hegemony; *ergo* it is proven that the Czechoslovak elements are a part of the international (U.S.) capitalist conspiracy. This is so because "everyone knows where attempts to undermine the forces for progress in various parts of the world originate from. . . ." [22] There is but one interlocking, international capitalist conspiracy and any deviation from orthodoxy is a manifestation of it.

Both the United States and the Soviet Union had considerable difficulty getting beyond this *ex hypothesi* level of proof for their contention that the nations they had just invaded were in reality being saved from an international conspiracy. The United States tried naming a handful of Communists among the Dominican revolutionaries. Russia discovered a small-arms cache of Western origins in Bohemia and named some Czechoslovakians who were allegedly fascists or agents of Western imperialism.[23] But, like the U.S. leaders, the Russians spoke mostly in assertions that compensated for lack of evidence by sheer immoderation. "The Soviet Union has irrefutable data," Mr. Malik said, "that events in Czechoslovakia can be traced outside that country. There is a dangerous conspiracy of the forces of internal and external reaction to restore the order which had been brought down by the

20. J. Malik, Security Council, 21 August 1968, S/PV.1441, p. 32.
21. *Ibid.*, pp. 43–45.
22. *Ibid.*, p. 46.
23. J. Malik, Security Council, 23 August 1968, S/PV.1443, pp. 82–95.

popular revolution." [24] It is difficult not to compare the words to those of Under Secretary Thomas C. Mann: "All those in our government who had full access to official information were convinced that the landing of additional troops was necessary in view of the clear and present danger of the forcible seizure of power by the Communists." Mr. Mann also stated that evidence indicated that para-military forces under the control of the Communists "exceeded" the strength of non-Communist rebel forces and that indeed these non-Communist rebels "were working hand in glove with the Communists." [25] But such evidence for the most part did not come to be revealed, and what there was did not support the sweeping conclusions drawn. In both instances, the superpowers found themselves scraping the bottom of the evidentiary barrel. U.S. spokesmen had to resort to evidence that certain Dominican leaders had received training in Communist countries or had traveled abroad or had been "inspired" by Cuba, Russia, or China. The Soviet Union found that the Czechoslovak reactionary leaders were being "influenced" by "American Press, television and radio—these mass media used the whole arsenal of misinformation, slander, calumny in interpreting the events in Czechoslovakia in a determined direction, incitement to further undermining the socialist order in Czechoslovakia." [26]

The United States may have refined the disingenuous concept of "vicarious aggression" during the Dominican invasion, but the Soviets used it repeatedly to show that their troops in Czechoslovakia were only engaging in collective self-defense. The Warsaw powers were members of a family of nations acting in concert to protect one of their own against those in the enemy camp who were "inciting the antisocialist elements in Czechoslovakia." [27]

What emerges from all this rhetoric is more than a distorted

24. J. Malik, Security Council, 21 August 1968, S/PV.1441, pp. 103–05.
25. The Hon. Thomas C. Mann, Department of State Press Release 241, Address before the Annual Meeting of the Inter-American Press Association, San Diego, Calif., October 12, 1965, pp. 9–10.
26. J. Malik, Security Council, 21 August 1968, S/PV.1441, p. 118.
27. *Ibid.,* pp. 119–20.

set of verbal echoes, or a record of lies, half-truths, and hypocrisy. Much more striking than whether there was "vicarious aggression" in the Dominican Republic and not in Czechoslovakia, or the other way around, is that both the United States and the Soviet Union appear to agree that "vicarious aggression" is justification for armed counterintervention. Even if the alleged facts in each instance were true, it makes no less horrendous the principles invented to link these so-called facts in a causal chain of deductive logic to the actions taken by a superpower. If a man asserts the right to kill anyone with red hair, it makes little difference whether a particular victim actually did have red hair. So, too, it matters little whether a superpower is right or wrong in alleging that Czechoslovak or Dominican leaders received moral support or were inspired by an ideology, propaganda, or education from outside their country; even if they had, the real issue is whether a superpower should in principle have the right to use force to remove such leaders from the government of a sovereign state on the ground that the state needs to be defended against the "vicarious aggression" of its own leaders. If this principle is mutually conceded, all attempts to distinguish between "real" and "false" vicarious aggression are, in any case, doomed to failure. Metaphors are notoriously subjective. Vicarious aggression is not aggression in an objective sense, but exists in the subjectivity of a beholder. It all depends on how sensitive, how vulnerable, how paranoid a superpower is; what on one occasion may be shrugged off as nuisance propaganda can on another be "vicarious aggression." There cannot be objective standards for defining so subjective a circumstance.

Those who try to base their use of force on a concept of self-defense against something less than the "armed attack" required by the charters of the U.N., the OAS, and even the Warsaw Pact, embark on a road full of logical conundrums, leading inevitably to the complete repeal of U.N. Charter Article 2(4)'s prohibition against the use of force in interstate relations. The further they stray from the relatively objective concept of armed attack into metaphoric nonevents like "vicarious," "constructive," or "apprehended" aggression, the larger these conundrums become. It may well be that the concept of "armed aggression" needs rethinking and reform to take into account the contemporary fashion for indirect aggression, whether by CIA or by "liberation" armies. But to speak of "vicarious aggression" or "foreign inspiration" as if these were armored divisions or foreign agents is not a helpful start. An example of how subjective and farfetched the concept of vicarious aggression can become was provided by Ambassador Malik, who told the Security Council as his nation's troops were consolidating their hold on Czechoslovakia, "What, if not open incitement, is the statement made on 28 April of this year by Eugene Rostow, Assistant Secretary of State, who said that the United States followed the events in Czechoslovakia with sympathy and hope?" And, Malik added petulantly, "This was only three months ago." [28] It is on such "instructions and directives from abroad" [29] that Czechoslovak anti-Communists relied to play "the role of imperialist agents in that country." [30] Behind their "counterrevolutionary activity one feels the directing hand of imperialist quarters" [31] and "the hallmarks of the C.I.A., the fingerprints of the C.I.A. . . ." [32]

The evidence presented before the U.N to the effect that certain Czechoslovaks were "vicarious aggressors" for the West discourages any faith in principles in international conduct based on such subjective standards. Thus we find it solemnly revealed that there was a general who "was a great friend of the British ambassador," a young man who was "the son of a former Minister of the Bohemian Moravian Protectorate" and another "whose father at present heads the reactionary organization, the Council of Free Czechoslovakia, in the United States." [33] Their

28. *Ibid.,* p. 121.
29. J. Malik, Security Council, 22 August 1968, S/PV.1442, p. 37.
30. *Ibid.*
31. J. Malik, Security Council, 21 August 1968, S/PV.1441, p. 131.
32. J. Malik, Security Council, 23 August 1968, S/PV.1443, p. 96.
33. *Ibid.,* p. 86.

offense was to belong to the "231 Club." This was the extent of the Soviet charges against these Czechoslovaks and the total evidence of their being agents of Western "vicarious aggression." Through these men the U.S. government sought

> to undermine and sap the socialist system and the socialist countries and create a breach in the socialist community. The imperialist circles of the United States, by political and ideological means involving secret, clandestine and subversive measures, stubbornly continue trying to tear apart the socialist community, to break its unity and weaken its ability to confront direct aggression.[34]

Readers will have to judge for themselves as best they can whether Ambassador Stevenson's recital of evidence of foreign intervention—direct, indirect, and vicarious—in 1965 [35] is more persuasive than that of Ambassador Malik in 1968. But it is quite clear that the verbal strategy of the two men at different times led them to espouse the same principle: the world (in the words of the U.S. representative) "must take into account the modern day reality that an attempt by a conspiratorial group, *inspired from outside,* to seize control by force can be an assault upon the independence and integrity of a state." [36] In other words, the United States and Russia have both asserted the principle that they may each decide at their own discretion to use force in a neighboring state when certain internal forces within that nation, "inspired" by an "alien" power or philosophy, appear to be taking control, even though the only external element is ideas, ideology, propaganda, and perhaps moral or even financial support. What makes this significant is that it is virtually inconceivable that a meaningful revolution or even a significant evolution such as was taking

34. *Ibid.,* p. 91.
35. Security Council Authorizes U.N. Representative in Dominican Republic. Statements made in the U.N. Security Council by U.S. Representative Adlai E. Stevenson. United States, Department of State, *Bulletin,* LII, 1965, pp. 869–85.
36. *Ibid.,* pp. 882–83. (Italics added.)

place in Czechoslovakia under Dubcek could occur in modern times without some such tenuous connection to the outside world, or without at least a suspicion of it. The U.S. and the Soviet verbal strategies in 1965 and 1968 come to no less than the assertion of an unlimited right to reverse, by military occupation if necessary, any substantial social, economic, and political change in any of the states belonging to their sphere of influence.

Taken together, this has two important transformational impacts on the system. First, it has the procedural effect of instituting a mutually recognized right to intervene in another state to defend it against a nonmilitary "attack." This could become tantamount to legitimized paranoia in international relations. Like paranoia, it makes irrelevant all external or objective reality. While the rule of the U.N., OAS, and Warsaw Pact charters limiting collective self-defense to instances of "armed attack" may be incomplete, it must be seriously questioned whether this amendment is one which is in our self-interest. Second, substantively, the effect of the new principles is to conduce to a freezing of the international *status quo* within the American and Soviet blocs. Aside from legal and political problems of implementation, such a freeze is not exactly life-affirming in its attitude toward change and human development. The United States public and leaders need to consider carefully whether they have wittingly or unwittingly become parties to such an agreement and whether they wish to continue the agreement and the legitimate expectations of the other side that such an agreement exists.

That the Soviet Union does believe an agreement to exist is indicated by their conduct and rhetoric during the Czechoslovak crisis. The U.S. government had claimed at the time of the Cuban and Dominican episodes that its use of force constituted an exercise in collective self-defense by the region against an alien incursion. The Soviets claimed no less for themselves:

> The decision of the socialist countries to give assistance to the Czechoslovak people is fully consonant with the right of peoples to individual and collective self-defence—a right

provided for in the Charter of the United Nations and in treaties of alliance concluded among fraternal socialist States. This is in conformity with, among others, the provisions of the Warsaw Pact.[37]

In fact, of course, the Warsaw Pact permits nothing of the sort, no more than does the Bogota Charter; nor would any sovereign state ever conceivably sign over such a right as is claimed by Russia and the United States, no matter how familial the relationship. But it is difficult to fault the Russians for the accuracy with which they picked up and employed in their own favor the principles conceived by leaders and spokesmen of the United States.

Similarly, the Soviets in 1968 felt free to argue, just as we did in the Guatemalan, Cuban, and Dominican crises, that their act of intervention and use of force were appropriate concerns not of the United Nations but only of the same regional body that had associated itself with the action. With scorn, Ambassador Malik spoke of the "imaginary and unfounded character of the requests tending to involve the Security Council in the question of Czechoslovakia since this is an utterly internal affair of the Czechoslovak Socialist Republic and the common cause and affair of its partners in the socialist community under the Warsaw Treaty." [38] Such "problems can be settled by the Czechoslovak people and Party and the sound forces in that country, with the support of the fraternal socialist States, and without the participation of the Security Council. . . ." [39] Ambassador Stevenson's approach during the Dominican Crisis was only slightly more muted:

> . . . the Security Council should not seek to duplicate or interfere with actions through regional arrangements. . . . The purpose of the United Nations Charter will hardly be served if two international organizations are seeking to do things in the same place with the same people at the same time.[40]

37. J. Malik, Security Council, 21 August 1968, S/PV.1441, p. 41. See also S/PV.1445, 24 August 1968, pp. 98–100.
38. J. Malik, Security Council, 21 August 1968, S/PV.1441, p. 101.
39. *Ibid.*, pp. 126–27.
40. A. Stevenson, Security Council, 1216th Mtg., 22 May 1965, p. 7.

It accrues somewhat to the credit of the United States that it permitted a U.N. presence to be established in the Dominican Republic, something the U.S.S.R. has refused not only in the case of its Czechoslovak but also its Hungarian interventions. But it was a grudging, minimal concession we made. Again, it must seriously be considered whether it is in the self-interest of the United States to continue to advocate the exclusion of United Nations organs from active participation in disputes between a great power and a small member of its "community."

The parallel continues. We argued in the Cuban and Dominican crises that our use of force was designed to perpetuate a precarious balance of power which would have been upset by the new developments in the Caribbean. So we could scarcely have been surprised to hear the Russians tell us in 1968, as they secured their interests on the banks of the Moldau, that "changes in the balance of forces in Europe would at the present time be an extremely serious threat to the security of peoples" [41] and that the "threat to the socialist system in Czechoslovakia is, at the same time, a threat to the foundations of European peace. This is why the actions of the Soviet Union and other socialist countries are motivated by a desire to strengthen peace and not to tolerate the undermining of the mainstays of European security." [42] Or, more expressly: "Of course, the latest events in Czechoslovakia have not only given rise to danger to the existing socialist system . . . there, but also are a direct threat to the violation of the existing balance of forces in Europe in favour of imperialism, which would inescapably subvert not only peace in Europe, but also threaten the security of the world as a whole." [43] Again, it is for us now seriously to consider whether the peace of the world we seek through the conduct of U.S. foreign relations is to be one built upon mutual support for this balance of forces. If we really believe democracy to be the more dynamic system, it would be to our interest to promote open ideological competition and trade in

41. J. Malik, Security Council, 21 August 1968, S/PV.1441, pp. 123–25.
42. *Ibid.,* pp. 38–40.
43. *Ibid.,* pp. 106–07.

ideas rather than to shelter vast land areas behind barriers erected against "alien" ideologies. It would be to our advantage, if we believe liberty rather than totalitarianism to be the dynamic force, to avoid endorsing a static balance of power.

After President Johnson declared on May 2, 1965, that "we in this hemisphere must . . . use every resource to prevent the establishment of another Cuba in this hemisphere," could the United States be surprised when Russia said "No more Titos"? While Tito remains a Communist, as did Dubcek, any deviation towards humanization and freedom constitutes a far greater threat to the brittle structure of the Soviet establishment than does Castro to the more flexible system of the United States. Is it therefore to our advantage to agree to a superpower system which allows the United States and the U.S.S.R. equally to suppress dissent within their zones of primacy? Yet since we asserted our right and that of the American states to use force to preserve the integrity of the Western Hemisphere's boundaries against Communist incursion, can we really complain when Ambassador Malik asserts that the "Soviet Union and other socialist countries in the interests of their security and the maintenance of international peace, could not but show their concern for the protection of the western borders of Czechoslovakia, which are the western borders of the community of all socialist states, of all States members of the Warsaw Pact." [44] Do we and the Russians not have a "deal"?

In virtually every other aspect of their verbal strategy and with uncanny faithfulness of detail, the Warsaw Pact nations employed the rhetoric of the United States during the crisis of August 1968. We sent troops into the Dominican Republic in a humanitarian effort to preserve law and order? Russia intervened in Czechoslovakia because "enemies were . . . shaking the foundations of law and order and . . . trampling laws underfoot . . . preparing to seize power." [45] The goal of the Warsaw Pact occupation was Czechoslovakia's "normalization." [46] We have already

44. *Ibid.*, pp. 123–25.
45. J. Malik, Security Council, 24 August 1968, S/PV.1445, pp. 118–20.
46. "Czechoslovakia," *New Times*, 35, September 4, 1968, p. 2.

noted that this was also the standard of the OAS regime in the Dominican Republic, which sought only "the return to normality." [47] Our sole objective in the Dominican Republic was to see that "the people of that country . . . freely choose the path of political democracy, social justice and economic progress." [48] Theirs in Czechoslovakia was solely "to clean up the atmosphere . . . and to create the necessary calm and serenity to allow the Czechoslovak people to put order in their home." [49] And once again the question is less whether our intentions were sincere and theirs hypocritical than whether military intervention should ever be justified in such terms, even when sincerely meant; whether this is the kind of normative, reciprocally applied system of superpower interaction and world order we want to join in building.

47. Second Report of the Special Committee of the Tenth Meeting of Consultation of Ministers of Foreign Affairs, Doc. 81, p. 7. U.N. Doc. S/6370, May 19, 1965.
48. President Johnson, Statement of May 1, 1965. United States, Department of State, *Bulletin,* LII, 1965, p. 743.
49. M. Tarabanov, Security Council, 23 August 1968, S/PV.1443, p. 146.

7

Words and Acts:
The False Dichotomy

THE TWO-GHETTO SYSTEM: COSTS AND BENEFITS

The principles of conduct formulated and enunciated by the verbal strategy of the U.S. government during the Guatemalan situation of 1954, in the Cuban missile crisis of 1962, and in the Dominican intervention of 1965 have now been confirmed by the Soviet invasion of Czechoslovakia as an applied doctrine of world order. By our verbal behavior, we enunciated principles of a world in which superpowers are licensed to operate ghettos of subservient states. By invading Czechoslovakia, Moscow has agreed to these principles. This acceptance does not necessarily make the Johnson-Brezhnev principles a permanent or irreversible basis for world order. Rather, a foundation has been laid, as the preceding chapter suggests, but the cement has not hardened.

There are, of course, things to be said for a two-ghetto system, which is a legitimating arrangement making Latin America, or in any event the Central American and Caribbean portions of it, subservient to the overriding interests of the United States, and Eastern Europe subservient to the Soviet Union. First, it may be argued that such an arrangement protects the national interest of the United States by excluding communism from the hemisphere and preserving established U.S. economic and military interests in the Americas. Second, the two-ghetto system, by drawing a line between "theirs" and "ours," might help stabilize the world political system and perhaps reduce cold-war tensions. Once the line between "theirs" and "ours" is firmly delimited, then perhaps, in Seyom Brown's words, a "period of peaceful competition, based initially on well-defined and mutually respected spheres of control, might *eventually* lead to . . . a less rigid international order." If we and the Soviets no longer felt our ultimate control threatened, perhaps we would both be inclined to relax certain rigid policies towards our respective regions. Third, it may be argued that since the Soviet Union will in any event keep Eastern Europe ghettoized, the United States must do the same in Latin America lest the world balance of power be upset.[2] Fourth, it is conceivable that the propensity for troublemaking by small states that are dependents of the superpowers is such that if the Great Powers are not to be dragged into dangerous squabbles, each must maintain strict discipline over its dependents.

Each of these is an arguable though in our opinion, unproven, proposition. On the other side it can equally be asserted that the growth of the bloc system has not so far led either to a reduction in interbloc tension or to intrabloc liberalization. However, the case against a two-ghetto system does not turn on the validity or invalidity of these assertions but on the cost of maintaining a U.S. hegemony in the Americas over a protracted period. It would be enormously expensive in purely military-economic terms, let alone in prestige and goodwill. But there would be even more prohibitive costs. If we were to subscribe to the principle of a two-ghetto system, we would further be blurring the line between U.S. democracy and Soviet communism. John N. Plank, scarcely a "soft" strategist, has warned that "if the United States loses its

1. Brown, *op. cit.*, p. 243.
2. For a further discussion of these advantages and disadvantages cf., R. N. Rosecrance, "Bipolarity, Multipolarity, and the Future" in 10 *Journal of Conflict Resolution* (1966), pp. 313–27.

identification with the concepts of political democracy, social justice, economic well-being and the dignity of the individual, it [will have] lost its purchase in this hemisphere." 3/As in Claudel's *jeu de cartes* in *Jeanne d'Arc au Bucher—"j'ai gagné, je veux dire que j'ai perdu"* (our gains would be our losses). And the essential differences between us and the Russians would lose credibility not only in this hemisphere but elsewhere as well. That would be a high cost, indeed, for a Pyrrhic victory.

Perhaps most important of all, citizens and strategists in the United States must also calculate the cost to the quality of life in their own country. It must at least be asked whether a people can long endure a double life of democracy at home and despotism abroad. History indicates that nations, like individuals, must seek an integrated life-style. This poses no present dilemma to Soviet authorities. The suppression of Czechoslovakia was readily paralleled by a revival of political and cultural despotism at home. The tap of repression still turns readily in modern Russia. But for the United States, a policy of regional repression would almost certainly create social and political conflicts at home that could end only in the restoration of democratic ideals to our foreign policy or else in a domestic regime as authoritarian as any we might impose on the hemisphere.

Given the prevalent democratic trend of political ethos in the United States, it seems unlikely that a sweeping policy of ruthless regional domination can find a permanent place in U.S. foreign policy. And unless such a policy is followed ruthlessly and consistently, it cannot be effective. It is far more likely that Russia can persist with a Brezhnev Doctrine than that the United States will persevere with the Johnson Doctrine. From the point of view of U.S. self-interest, therefore, the bargain struck, intentionally or unintentionally, by the confluence of the Johnson and Brezhnev doctrines is a bad one. It appears to give our joint blessing to a policy that Russia is much more likely to pursue

3. John N. Plank, "The Caribbean: Intervention, When and How" 44 *Foreign Affairs* 35 (1965), p. 48.

consistently than we, and from which they are therefore likely to derive far greater benefit. Without our doctrinal blessing, the Soviets might still periodically invade their Eastern European vassal states, but at least we would not be helping to lower the cost of such actions.

THE ROLE OF ENUNCIATED CONCEPTS, PRINCIPLES, AND DOCTRINES

It is as a matter, not only of moral altruism but also of national self-interest, that we judge the two-ghetto system a bad bargain. But can there be said to have been a bargain at all? The fact that both countries have stated their respective regional policies in virtually identical terms is certainly significant. But how significant? How important a factor in world politics are words, principles, and doctrines? What weight should be attributed to what states say? There are many Americans inside and outside government who regard verbal strategy as very much on the fringes of national policy. It is fashionable for "hardheaded realists," a category of intellect much prized in government, to discount words and principles. Words arc weaklings, principles are "just hot air," and what is said is rarely meant or believed by speaker or listener. By deeds alone do we know and are we known. "Deeds, not words shall speak me" as the sixteenth-century poet Beaumont said.

This scorn for verbal conceptualization in international politics is a persistent and widely shared folly. A far more accurate assessment is that of Richard Rovere:

> If it were always possible to distinguish between words and deeds, this would be a splendid and time-saving rule for political scientists and for all long-suffering citizens of this or any other government, and widespread appreciation and application of it would lead—no doubt beneficially—to much bureaucratic unemployment and to thinner newspapers. However, words often do have consequences ("Bombs away!"),

and though there is frequently a disparity between what governments say and what they do, what they say is generally to be regarded as part of what they do—and, at times, the more important part.[4]

Verbal weapons are as "real" in their strategic potential as missiles and submarines. As long as this is not understood, the United States will continue to be maneuvered into strategic positions it need not have taken and which are not in its national interest. We cannot know where we and the Soviets stand in relation to each other and to the states in our region, let alone how we might initiate a change in that stance, until we rid ourselves of cultural preconceptions about a dichotomy between words and deeds and learn to appreciate the importance of a strategy of verbal behavior.

The position is correctly stated by Professor Stanley Hoffmann: "The distinction between acts and verbal policies is losing its usefulness." [5] In an era of overkill and nuclear balance of terror, the "importance of signals, messages, communications in

---

4. Richard Rovere, "Letter from Washington," *The New Yorker,* July 12, 1969, p. 69. Fortunately, a new wave of observers of international politics are beginning to discuss the importance of verbal strategy in the context of the "credibility gap" separating the U.S. government and the American people. Mr. Thomas L. Hughes, the newly installed President of the Carnegie Endowment for International Peace, devoted his entire inaugural address to the subject. Anthony Lake, a foreign policy adviser to Senator Edmund Muskie, also discussed the issue in an article titled "Lying Around Washington," *Foreign Policy,* No. 2, Spring 1971, pp. 91–113. Both authors assert that the predominant tendency of public officials to publicly obfuscate issues is beginning to seriously undermine the democratic process. In Hughes's words, "The confidence of the country has collapsed in part precisely because of the degree and number of options which the President and his advisors apparently think must be reserved for his own last clear chance judgments in conducting foreign policy." Lake's article includes an analysis of the pressures in government which support this tendency and provides a series of concrete suggestions as to how to deal with them

5. Stanley Hoffmann, *Gulliver's Troubles, Or the Setting of American Foreign Policy,* New York: McGraw-Hill for the Council on Foreign Relations, 1968, p. 63.

bargaining situations like today's (marked by mixed interest and limited force) implies that verbal policies are indeed policies and tantamount to acts insofar as they affect an opponent's understanding of a nation's attitude and reactions." [6] Or, as Emerson said in *The Poet,* "Words are also actions, and actions are a kind of words."

Verbal strategy should be part of all strategic thinking and planning. Verbalized concepts are strategically important in two ways. Any deployment of words by a state is likely to have some effect on (1) *the international system in general* and (2) *the options available to the state in further specific confrontations with other states.*

A verbal strategy is as important as military strategy. This is a conclusion not to be found in the traditional texts—certainly not in Clausewitz, not even in Mattingly, Nicolson, or Lauterpacht. It grows out of a whole new strategic science of the nuclear age, which has established that:

• Force is deployed and made credible in order not to have to be employed.

• Every action by one nuclear superpower can be stopped by another superpower; thus no action by one superpower is possible without some acquiescence by the other.

• This acquiescence cannot be compelled by military force alone, since each superpower has the potential to destroy the other and is thus the military equal of the other.

• Nevertheless, superpowers can score gains in international politics. Interaction between nations is not a "zero-sum" game— the amount of gain by one state is not necessarily in direct ratio to the amount of loss by the other. Thus the definition of victory in a crisis is not necessarily the defeat of an opponent. Verbal strategy plays an important role in this definition and thus in the achievement of victory.

• The opponent in each crisis is subject to persuasion that

6. *Ibid.,* p. 64; Hoffmann also suggests, correctly in our view, that "the ratio of purely verbal policies is extraordinarily high today in everyone's foreign policy."

he should not act. Verbal strategy has a role to play in this persuasion.

• All crises between states are subgames of a larger, continuing game. Thus the strategy of any subgame must be calculated by taking into account also the projected effect on the larger game.

• All states have an interest in the larger game which exceeds that in winning any particular subgame.

• The rules of the game of international politics are subject to change in accordance with the way each subgame is played. Such changes may significantly influence the outcome of future subgames.

These rules of the new strategy are designed for a world in which at least two states have more power than has ever been possessed by any state previously and are predominant over all other states in terms of military capability. In this new world, the two superpowers do not simply "cancel each other out." They create a wholly new condition of strategic interaction in which the role of force is still enormous even though it is immobilized, but in which new nonmilitary concepts—mutually shared expectations, images, climate, signals, patterns of behavior, and reciprocity—take on new strategic significance. It is in the management of these added factors that one superpower has an opportunity not to defeat but to outgain the other through skillful verbal strategy. Through carefully conceived verbal strategy, one superpower has the possibility of persuading or maneuvering the other into an acquiescence.

CHOICE OF VERBAL STRATEGY AND LEVELS
OF INTENTIONALITY

Among reasonable men it is customary and, indeed, necessary to presume that a person means what he says. Where this presumption fails, the resultant loss of credibility shuts the disbelieved individual off from normal social intercourse and leads him and those with whom he deals to miscalculations and chaos. So, too, when a state speaks. If a national official, vested with the ostensible power to commit and bind his country, speaks in his formal capacity, others in the international community have a right to assume that he intends his words to be a deliberate expression of state policy. Like the individual, the official speaking for the state is expected to mean what he says—not simply whatever he thinks he means but what to the reasonable listener will be the logical concomitant of the words. The significance of words is not idiosyncratic but is derived from the consensual pattern of perceptual behavior in a community. Words are used in a cultural context, which governs their meaning. Youths who call policemen "pigs" in Chicago may engender resentment; but to call a policeman in Mecca "pig" would engender a wholly different level of reaction, whether the speakers intended the added level of sacrilege or not. In the community of states, when a nation speaks to explain why it is embarking on a course of action, it is ordinarily understood by other states also to be proposing a principle for future conduct or reinforcing an existing principle. Other states have a right to assume that the speaker knows and intends this level of his meaning and that he knows that the listening states make this assumption. On this shared mutual expectation rests the element of predictability that prevents relations between states in the nuclear era, particularly the superpowers, from being chaotic and far more dangerous than they usually are. Words play a key role in forming these shared mutual expectations, for even the simplest explanation contains elements of prediction when it is made by a state. For this reason, what is said plays an important role in determining the systemic and strategic interaction between states.

The verbal behavior of a state is seldom random. Almost always it is designed intentionally to advance the national interest. It is therefore a part of national strategy, intended like military or economic strategy, to produce certain predictable and desired effects. Problems arise when the national interest is not exhaustively defined by the speaker, when the verbal behavior is designed only with an eye to its effect on an immediate crisis, forgetting that the words do not cease to be systemically and strategically important once the crisis is over. For example, what U.S. leaders and representatives *said* during the Guatemalan, Cuban-missile, and Dominican crises was undoubtedly intended to make these specific U.S. actions appear at the moment in the most favorable possible light. The verbal strategy of the United States was conceived to make our actions appear to opponents, friends, and neutrals in such a way as would induce them to cooperate with us or in any event not to hinder the achievement of our immediate goal. Insofar as the verbal behavior served this short-range strategy, it was deemed appropriate. Apparently almost forgotten were the other levels of meaning, the logical concomitants, and their impact on longer-range strategic interests.

Yet those long-term interests may be by far the more important. A strategy of verbal behavior that fails to keep this longer range of impact in focus can be costly, no matter how successful it is in helping win any single strategic encounter; for when a state, particularly a superpower like the United States, speaks, its words affect not only those specific events to which they are addressed, but also the international system as a whole and, thus, the options available in a subsequent crisis. Whether a particular explanation of a specific action is to the national interest thus depends on more than whether it is a "good cover."

Successful verbal strategy is the selection of what is said so that the intended immediate effect is achieved but in which the longer-run systemic effect is also intended and successfully accomplished. Professor Roger Fisher points out the need to keep in mind these two different levels of intention [7]: "the United States' basic objectives are: first, to win each dispute with another country and, second, to avoid war and develop a fair way of settling such disputes" or in other words, there is an interest both "in winning

---

7. Roger Fisher, "Fractionating Conflict," in Fisher (ed.), *International Conflict and Behavioral Science,* New York: Basic Books, 1964, p. 94.

each case and in promoting the rule of law—a regime in which the government does not always win." Fisher rightly notes that these objectives can be "somewhat inconsistent" because, while "the United States would like to win *each* dispute, it is not seeking a world in which any one country wins every dispute." Or in Dean Pruitt's terms, the "players" must keep in mind their interest not only in each "interaction between two players on a single issue" but also in "the broader picture." The participants must remember that "the sum total of all the individual games played by two players can be thought of as a *larger game*. . . ." [8] Thus the player in planning his strategy for one single subgame must avoid anything that wins the single encounter but loses other, more important subgames or contributes to his losing or to the other party's leaving the larger game.

What this suggests is both a different approach to conceptualizing verbal strategy and to accounting the costs of any single subgame. Strategic planning must proceed from the axiom that nothing should be said in any crisis, no matter how "persuasive" in the circumstances, which could later be applied in other circumstances by the Soviet Union in a way likely to injure the interests of the United States. It is the role of the strategic planner to think ahead, to predict potential future crises, to project the effect of a proposed rationale in various future contingencies, and to reject a verbal strategy that would make for short-term gain but larger long-term loss. This means that he must operate strategically at each of the levels of intentionality. Similarly, in evaluating the costs and benefits to be derived from a single encounter it is essential not merely to predict who will "win" but also to estimate which moves, including verbalization of supportive concepts, will be necessary to win and to calculate the cost of having these same concepts applied against us at a later time. It is not inconceivable that certain "victories" won by the United States would, by this method of accounting, show up as long-run defeats.

In seeking to advance the national interest, those planning

8. Dean G. Pruitt, "An Analysis of Responsiveness Between Nations," 6 *Journal of Conflict Resolution* (1962), p. 10.

U.S. strategy, including our verbal strategy, must take into account not only the need to win specific encounters but also the national stake in a continuing, just, and effective international system. The verbal behavior which at one level conveniently appears to justify our conduct in a single crisis but which at another level helps to wreck the existing patterns of relations or introduces a new principle of interaction that may subsequently be employed by others to our disadvantage is verbal behavior not in the national interest.

When the President of the United States says in a speech to a group of U.S. bankers, "The liquidity of the international payments system requires consideration of an upward revaluation of the Deutschmark," he may be merely conveying an opinion for discussion by a group of professionals, or he may be trying to force the Germans to revalue, or he may primarily be asserting the power of the United States to regulate the world monetary system. Whether the particular speech is sound verbal strategy depends, in the first instance, upon whether its level of effect corresponds with its level of intentionality. If the President merely intended to convey a tentative opinion for discussion, his verbal strategy is probably faulty. Unless timing, circumstance, or formulation clearly indicates otherwise, states are entitled to assume that the President is speaking from the highest level of intentionality, that his purpose includes system transformation.

Nor is it easy to indicate otherwise. Although it is sometimes difficult for our leaders to convey that they "mean business," it is even more difficult for them to convey that they do not. The international arena, like the stock market, can be sent into gyrations by the most offhand remark of a public official. Deliberately used, a gap between level of intentionality and level of effect can sometimes be an effective strategy. The press leak is employed this way, allowing an official to elicit maximum reaction to a proposal without finally being committed to it. But the same gap can de disadvantageous when it is inadvertent. Every man who in the fullness of a moment has said, "I love you," has learned that the words cannot but have longer-range system-transforming effect on the pattern of relations with the other person, even if they were only intended to have the limited short-run effect of flattering or seducing or otherwise managing an immediate crisis.

There are, broadly, three levels of intentionality in verbal behavior. At the upper level of the scale are statements made precisely to bring about broad system-transformation. Prime Minister Harold Macmillan's "winds of change" speech was an indirect but successful effort to change the whole structure of colonial relations and to replace it with a new pattern of self-determination. It was largely successful in this. The Truman Doctrine was equally high on the scale of intentionality, being a calculated signal of America's decision to become and remain an actor in the postwar European arena.

President Kennedy's *"Ich bin ein Berliner"* speech, on the other hand, may have had as its first priority the achievement of a more limited objective—reassuring the West Berlin population and warning the Russians at a moment of crisis that seizure of the city would not be tolerated. Such a crisis-management signal in concert with other consistent signals may nevertheless, over a period of time, succeed in transforming a whole pattern of interaction, instance by instance, or in reinforcing an existing pattern of conduct. Systemic change or systemic reinforcement may in such circumstances be a valuable by-product of crisis management. Or it may be unintended and unwelcome fallout, depending on the acuity of the verbal strategy being employed. For example, when certain of President Kennedy's former advisers presume, a decade after the *"Ich bin ein Berliner"* speech, to criticize West German Chancellor Willy Brandt, the former mayor of Berlin, for softness toward the Russians, it may be that they are still being more Berliner than the Berliners, transforming a statement made by the President to help manage a single crisis into a continuing systemic relationship that makes the United States rather than Bonn the principal watchdog responsible for the foreign policy of the German Federal Republic.

At the bottom of the scale of intentionality is a statement intended neither to affect the system nor to induce the listener to any immediate course of conduct. Such purely informational verbal behavior, if it is not to sow confusion and precipitate unwanted results, must be clearly labeled. Even then, it is likely to be misunderstood, so that persons possessing the ostensible power to "commit or bind" should generally eschew public speech of low-level intentionality.

This low-level range of verbal behavior is, however, often the one at which a statement is aimed. It includes remarks made solely to present in the most favorable possible light an action a state has taken or is contemplating without intending either strategic or systemic effect. Statements in this category are intended as exercises in apologetics. Too frequently, however, these exercises are dismissed, in the minds of the policy planners where they originate, as "window dressing" or "propaganda"—mere words that quickly die away and are devoid of strategic significance. But this is to misperceive, perhaps dangerously, their latent effect on listeners and on systems. The records of U.N. debates are full of apologetics of low-level intentionality which are meant only to put a good face on some action already taken. Unfortunately, although apologetics are verbal behavior at lowest-level intentionality, this cannot be admitted at the time without loss of propaganda impact. Others are entitled to assume a higher level of intentionality. The Russians' use of our prior rhetoric during the 1968 Czechoslovak events is a dramatic instance of what happens when apologetics— ours in this instance—do not proceed from a soundly conceived verbal strategy that takes into account the possibility that other states may treat what we say more seriously than we do ourselves.

INTERNATIONAL SYSTEM AND SYSTEM TRANSFORMATION

The strategic planner whose task it is to choose the verbal strategy to accompany an act must calculate the total aggregate of consequences, those for the immediate, present management of the interaction and those of the future. To be able to do this he must understand the functioning of *system* in the relations between states and especially, if he is an American, between the United States and the Soviet Union.

There are probably almost as many definitions of international system as there are political scientists, and few mountains have been described from so many different vantages with such varying results. Raymond Aron, for example, takes the view that the international system is an "ensemble constituted by political units that maintain regular relations with each other and that are all capable of being implicated in a generalized war." [9] Stanley Hoffmann describes international system as a "pattern of relations between the basic units of world politics which is characterized by the scope of the objectives pursued by those units and of the tasks performed among them, as well as by the means used in order to achieve those goals and perform those tasks." [10] According to Charles Hermann, "a system is a set of actors (for example, nations, international organizations, and so on) interacting with one another in established patterns and through designated structures." [11] All of these definitions, despite their variations, have in common a recognition of what Wolfram Hanreider calls "an indispensable attribute of systems," namely, "behavioral regularity, which is the basis for establishing relational patterns or structures." [12] Morton Kaplan also emphasizes that a "pattern of repeatable or characteristic behavior does occur within the international system." [13]

For the purposes of this study, the international system con-

9. Raymond Aron, *Peace and War: A Theory of International Relations*, Garden City, N. J.: Doubleday & Co., 1966, p. 94. (Italics omitted.)
10. Stanley Hoffmann, "International Systems and International Law," 14 *World Politics* (October 1961), p. 207.
11. Charles F. Hermann, "International Crisis as a Situational Variable," in James N. Rosenau (ed.), *International Politics and Foreign Policy: Reader in Research and Theory*, New York: The Free Press, 1969, p. 411.
12. Wolfram F. Hanreider, "The International System: Bipolar or Multibloc?" 9 *Journal of Conflict Resolution* (1965), p. 300.
13. Morton A. Kaplan, "Variants on Six Models of the International System," in Rosenau, *op. cit.*, p. 291.

sists of the stable patterns of interactions among states. Where a stable pattern of conduct operates among all or most states, the term "system" is used. Where the pattern of consistent interaction is one that relates only to a part of the international community— the OAS or the nuclear superpowers, for example—we use the term "subsystem." Thus, the term "international system" is best reserved for a framework of patterned universal interaction, while more specialized patterns of relationship that apply only to two or a few states we shall call subsystems.[14]

Where we speak of the "systemic effect" of verbal strategy or the impact of a state's verbal strategy on the "international system," we mean to call attention to the implications of what a state is saying on those relatively fixed patterns of interaction that have come to be expected and accepted in relations between states— whether, in other words, a strategy tends to proceed along a well-worn track formed by previous conduct or cuts the beginnings of a track of its own.

Cutting a track of one's own changes the landscape on which initiatives, strategy, and interaction can occur. A new path may be followed by others and may gradually obliterate older tracks. This capacity of one innovation to initiate changes in an entire pattern of behavior, we refer to as its potential for system transformation. Every instance of behavior by a superpower contains a significant potential for system confirmation—supporting existing patterns of interaction—or for system transformation—changing the patterns. Words define state action. The verbal strategy of a superpower in a specific crisis, even if meant only to justify one instance of conduct, can be picked up by the other side and used in reciprocal circumstances to its own advantage. In this sense, all that is said to explain a single act has systemic consequences which ought to be foreseen. As former Assistant Secretary of State Richard N.

14. For a definition of *arena,* used to refer to nonsystemic interaction contexts," see Harold D. Lasswell, "The Climate of International Action," in Herbert C. Kelman, *International Behavior: A Social-Psychological Analysis,* New York: Holt, Rinehart and Winston, 1965, p. 341.

Gardner has observed, "The law you make may be your own." If a superpower successfully asserts a rule of conduct in explaining its actions and that rule is subsequently applied advantageously by a second superpower, the first is at a strategic disadvantage by reason of the second's assumption that its course of conduct will not be impeded. The rule asserted by the first superpower becomes a shield against deterrence. Understanding the systemic effects of a state's conceptualization of its conduct is a necessary component to the construction of an effective deterrent strategy. For example, it ought to have been recognized that when President Johnson explained our invasion of the Dominican Republic in terms of a doctrine of limited sovereignty and regional self-defense against an alien ideology he in effect offered the Soviets the right to depose any regime in Eastern Europe that appeared to threaten socialist orthodoxy. In August 1968 the "offer" was accepted. Strategically it means little to argue—however true—that we did not intend this systemic consequence. We knew, and the Russians knew that we knew, that the Brezhnev Doctrine was the reciprocal of the Johnson Doctrine. Estoppel in such circumstances is not merely a legal but also a systemic and strategic concept.

The notion that something one superpower has previously asserted by word and/or deed tends to inhibit it from preventing the other superpower from subsequently asserting the same right is a manifestation of the idea of *reciprocity*. Reciprocity, the duty to give in equal or equivalent measure what one takes, is so ubiquitous a principle of interaction and so central to all systemic behavior that, whether or not U.S. spokesmen intended the principles they enunciated during the Guatemalan, Cuban, and Dominican crises to have reciprocal application for the Soviet Union, it should have been known to be virtually inevitable that they would do so.

The concept of reciprocity has long fascinated professional observers. High among the more interesting conceptual work is that of A. W. Gouldner. He makes three points essential to our argument: (1) some concept of reciprocity invariably appears in social arenas that achieve a high level of continuous interaction, (2) reciprocity serves as a starting mechanism transforming random interaction into systemic patterns, and (3) reciprocity functions, once the system is established, to reinforce systemic stability.[15] Gouldner cites Piaget,[16] Hobhouse,[17] Thurnwald,[18] Simmel,[19] Lévi-Strauss,[20] and Malinowski [21] for the proposition that reciprocity is a universal, and, in Hobhouse's words, "the vital principle of society." [22]

Reciprocal relations appear to originate as a ubiquitous social phenomenon in the exchange of equivalent benefits. A primitive fisherman gives fish to the craftsman for mending his nets. On another occasion, he trades fish to a farmer for vegetables. If these isolated transactions are mutually satisfactory, they may be repeated and in time become routinized behavior. Each separate reciprocal transaction will strengthen the routine. Gradually, adaptations in the routine may occur—in the ratio of fish to vegetables, for example. If the system of exchange, the routine, survives these adaptations, it may become more sophisticated. When his catch is small, the fisherman may give the net-mender a promissory note for later redemption. When the farmer's crop is unusually large, he may persuade the fisherman to buy more vegetables and to use the surplus to pay for net-mending. In time, the fisherman, net-mender

15. A. W. Gouldner, "The Norm of Reciprocity: A Preliminary Statement," 25 *American Sociological Review* (1960), p. 161.
16. Jean Piaget, *The Moral Judgment of the Child*, New York: Collier Books, 1962, pp. 199*ff.*
17. Gouldner, *loc. cit.*, p. 161, citing L. T. Hobhouse, *Morals in Evolution: A Study in Comparative Ethics*, London: Chapman & Hall, 1951, 1st edition, 1906, p. 12.
18. *Ibid.*, citing Richard Thurnwald, *Economics in Primitive Communities*, London: Oxford University Press, 1932, p. 106.
19. *Ibid.*, pp. 161–62, citing Georg Simmel, *The Sociology of Georg Simmel*, Kurt H. Wolff (ed.), Glencoe, Illinois: The Free Press, 1950, p. 387.
20. *Ibid.*, p. 162, citing Claude Lévi-Strauss, *Les Structures élémentaires de la parenté*, Paris: Les Presses Universitaires, 1949.
21. Gouldner cites the work of Malinowski throughout his paper; see esp. pp. 169–71, which cite Bronislaw Malinowski, *Crime and Custom in Savage Society*, London: Paul, Trench, Trubner, 1932.
22. *Ibid.*, p. 161.

and farmer may all come to realize that they have a stake not only in each individual reciprocal transaction, but in a general system of exchange in which benefits may be transferred, deferred, or averaged out. Eventually this general system or habitual pattern of interaction may itself come to be more valuable to the interactors than any single transaction between them. But it would take only a single, or a very few, important breaches of the rules of the exchange—a failure to redeem a promissory note or a careless job of net-mending, to bring this complex and beneficial system of relations to a halt. At this point, the role of reciprocity has changed from one that facilitates a single interaction to one that upholds the stability of the entire system of relations.

The principle of reciprocity thus extrapolates individual behavior into systemic transformation and facilitates not only business and trade but all those everyday accommodations that make societal living possible. Piaget identifies the point where a concept of reciprocity impinges on human consciousness as the beginning of the child's awareness of the notion of social contract. So, too, with states. Systemic development begins and behavior becomes patterned and predictable when states begin to comprehend that what they do and the principles upon which they proceed to act constitute offers to let other states conduct themselves reciprocally, by reference to the same principles. This especially applies today in superpower politics of peaceful coexistence. Moreover, states not directly affected by a single interaction have come to see themselves with a stake in the *pattern* of reciprocal superpower interactions. That is why the Yugoslav Government was moved by the Czechoslovak crisis of 1968 to warn that its "negative consequences will not only affect the Czechoslovak Socialist Republic, but also the interests and relations of other countries, their internal security and stability of peace in Europe and in the world." [23]

Reciprocity, therefore, is a factor essential to the emergence of structured, patterned, systemic behavior. Some element of systemic behavior is essential to survival in an age of nuclear weap-

23.   A. Vratusa, U.N. Doc. S/PV.1444, 23 August 1968, p. 56.

onry. There must be predictable patterns of systemic state behavior among the superpowers, if only to guard against war by miscalculation. This does not necessarily mean cooperation and harmony. Even a stable pattern of hostility among nuclear powers is likely to be more psychologically tolerable than one in which the interactions of the Soviet Union and the United States are entirely idiosyncratic. A system of shared mutual expectations about future conduct is also necessary to an effective strategy of deterrence. Countries at war, too, have common interests which they must seek to protect by behaving in accordance with mutually perceived reciprocal principles and by being able to rely on the enemy to act reciprocally in accordance with the same principles. Moreover, a hostile act by one superpower tends both to encourage and to free the other to behave similarly. When Secretary Dulles' adherence to cooperative principles of U.N. law at the time of the Suez crisis was countered by the Soviets' callous disregard for those same principles in the Hungarian invasion, the U.N. principles lost even more of whatever ability they still had to inhibit U.S. conduct. The U.S. use of force during the Cuban missile crisis was less risky and certainly less costly because the Soviet invasion of Hungary had helped pave the way toward its being systemic rather than idiosyncratic conduct.

Since, in serious encounters between superpowers, each nuclear nation has the ultimate power to prevent the other from achieving a stated policy goal, it is strategically important for the initiating state in any such encounter to convince its opponent that its interests do not warrant the escalation necessary to prevent the initiative from succeeding. One way to do this is to cast the initiative in enunciated terms of reciprocal application, terms which may be seen to be advantageous in the long run to both parties. It is easier to yield in a subgame without fighting, if the yielding party knows that this is being done within an ongoing system of interaction which assures that the interaction will continue and that there is a fair chance of winning a subsequent subgame by reciprocal operation of the same rules or enunciated principles. The gain-loss ratio in a retreat made under the aegis of a reciprocal principle is quite different from that in a defeat based solely on the enemy's successful idiosyncratic exertion of superior power. In the words of George Liska, "the final condition is habitual adjustment of conflicts in ways and on terms which are not humiliating for any one party—or at least not for the same party all or most of the time." [24] Adjustments made in accordance with enunciated principles within the framework of reciprocal systemic interaction are thus more likely to be successfully achieved without recourse to violence.

Reciprocity is strategically and systemically important not only in a continuing hostile relationship between states, but also in the development and reinforcement of patterns of cooperation. The process of moving from hostile to cooperative patterns of interaction, the ultimate objective of system stabilization, is likely to be facilitated where the interaction is systematized by normative reciprocity. Roger Fisher emphasizes this function of reciprocity in transforming conflict into cooperation:

> If we wish to win a controversy, it would seem wiser to say that the solution we seek is not only consistent with our principles but is also consistent with those of our adversary —at least if properly construed and applied. By insisting that our adversary can come along without abandoning his principles, we make it easier for him to do so.[25]

Ideally, he adds, "one country should yield on a dispute about which its adversary cares more than it does, confident that on some subsequent occasion the process would be reversed." [26] Confidence is the key; it is warranted only where the conduct of states conforms reciprocally to systemic patterns of interaction, thereby confirming mutually shared expectations. Confidence that a state means what it says can be of vast strategic benefit. But such

24. George Liska, *Imperial America,* Baltimore: Johns Hopkins Press, 1967, p. 31.
25. Fisher, *op. cit.,* p. 99.
26. *Ibid.,* p. 103.

confidence is practically impossible to establish unless a state may be taken to mean not only what it says, but all the rational concomitants of what it says. And of these, the most important is the reciprocal—that a principle the state asserts in one case will be applicable to similar future cases and that a right it asserts for itself is one it will also accord to others.

Development and stabilization of systemic interaction is therefore a part of any thoughtful definition of strategic self-interest. In the case of superpower relationships the minimal obligation is to act in accordance with the norm of reciprocity. In practical terms this means that U.S. policy making must generally accept the right of the Soviet Union to pursue reciprocal policies that are the equivalent of those being asserted by us. This suggests the importance of properly predicting the cost to the United States of a proposed policy—not only what it would cost us if we were to pursue it, but what it would cost us if we signaled thereby a willingness to allow our opponents to pursue that policy reciprocally.

By failing to take into account the reciprocal system-transforming effect of the principles we enunciate and by which we purport to act, by not "listening to ourselves as if we were the enemy speaking," we are likely to misperceive our opponents' strategic position, which in turn conduces to serious strategic miscalculations. Several theoretical strategists, including George Kennan,[27] Marshall Shulman,[28] and Zbigniew Brzezinski,[29] began to conclude by 1965 that the Soviet Union's rigid domination of a united international Communist movement was giving way, particularly in Eastern Europe, to a pluralistic, nationalistic pattern of socialist states relatively free to pursue their perceived self-interest.

27. George F. Kennan, *On Dealing with the Communist World*, New York: Harper & Row, 1964.
28. Marshall D. Shulman, *Beyond the Cold War*, New Haven: Yale University Press, 1966.
29. Zbigniew Brzezinski, *Alternative to Partition: For a Broader Conception of America's Role in Europe*, New York: McGraw-Hill, 1965.

None of these experts realized that our reassertion between 1960 and 1964 of a doctrine of bloc discipline applicable to Cuba and, particularly, to the Dominican Republic would help pave the way for its reciprocal reassertion by the Soviet Union within its own bloc.

To the degree a superpower fails to think reciprocally about its own behavior, it fails to be realistic in its understanding of how that behavior through the operation of mutually shared expectations and the systemic norm of reciprocity affects and alters the system. Such lack of realism is strategically self-defeating, for it leads to faulty planning in which probabilities and contingencies are miscalculated. Such miscalculations face the calculator with a sudden, painful choice—to permit the other side to make an unexpected gain or to violate the basic rule of the game, the systemic norm of reciprocity. Either way, the miscalculator loses. Had the United States denied the systemic effects of its prior actions and the verbal strategy by which those actions were presented to the community of states, had it in August 1968 threatened to use force if necessary to prevent the Soviets from asserting rights conceptually equivalent to those earlier asserted by us,[30] then it would have been seriously undermining the norm of reciprocity on which the international system is based. This would have been dangerous in that the survival of some element of system or of predictable patterns in the interaction between the superpowers is

30. What is an equivalent situation to which reciprocity applies? The question is discussed, and rules for determining equivalence are proposed, in an article by the authors which supplements this study: Franck and Weisband, "The Role of Reciprocity and Equivalence in Systemic Superpower Interaction," *New York University Journal of International Law and Politics*, 3, Winter 1970, No. 2, pp. 263–77. For a relevant discussion from the perspectives of legal philosophy see Paul W. Taylor, "Universalizability and Justice" in *Ethics and Social Justice*, Howard E. Kiefer and Milton K. Munitz (eds.), Albany, N.Y.: State University of New York Press, 1968, pp. 142–63; also consult A. W. Gouldner, *The Coming Crisis of Western Sociology*, New York: Basic Books, 1970, esp. pp. 231–45, for a discussion of some of the sociological implications.

to everyone's advantage, not least to the United States. In the summer of 1968, the Soviets were entitled under the rules of the system to assume that we would not use force to deny them recourse to their equivalent of the Johnson Doctrine. A sudden shift in signals and a repudiation of an implied reciprocal obligation on our part would have created an extremely serious crisis, perhaps pushing the world to the brink of nuclear war.

The Soviet leaders undoubtedly knew this and took it into account in calculating the probable risks and costs involved in their intended act. Their calculations were correct, even as those of our Kremlinologists had been wrong.[31] Presumably they had listened to us, and we had not.

31. Szulc, *op. cit.,* p. 399 declares, "I submit that a shock greater only than the invasion itself was, precisely, the lack of a reaction. The Soviet Union may have utterly misinterpreted the internal situation in Czechoslovakia . . . but it was absolutely correct in its assumption that the so-called Free World would accept the invasion with no more than pious expressions of regret and condemnation."

8

Verbal Strategy
of Hostility and Cooperation

VERBAL STRATEGY OF HOSTILITY: DETERRENCE

Patterns of interaction develop and play a role in both hostile
and friendly relations between states. Even where states, such as
the United States and the Soviet Union, habitually interact with
each other in a self-assertive, competitive manner, their hostile
relations evolve subsystemic rules of the game which regularize
the management of crises and thus help to prevent nuclear catastrophe.

In an ongoing hostile relationship, as in any other, the states
party to a series of confrontations must keep in mind the longer-
run subsystemic as well as the immediate crisis-managerial effects
of what they do, as well as what they say. The task of policy
strategists is to make the management of any particular crisis supportive of the general subsystemic norms, which, in turn, will be
helpful in the management of future crises.

Deterrence strategy is the process of developing important
systemic norms applicable to ongoing hostile relationships. Thomas
Schelling defines deterrence as being "concerned with influencing
the choices that another party will make, and doing it by influenc-

ing his expectations of how we will behave." [1] Its purpose is to ensure that both sides do not embark on initiatives which would inevitably lead the other to respond with military force. In the hostile subsystem of the nuclear superpowers, deterrence strategy is a prime factor in preventing all-out war by miscalculation.

In a world of mutually suspicious states, conflicting interests, and strong nationalisms, it is inevitable that international relations should be marked to some extent, by hostility. When that mutual hostility extends to the superpowers, their leaders have a common interest in managing hostile encounters in such a way as to protect and promote their interests and maximize their advantages without engendering a conflict in which both sides would lose. So long as hostility remains a feature of international relations, therefore, a rational strategy of hostility is also a part of the pursuit of peace.

At the core of a rational strategy of hostility is deterrence. Each superpower attempts to make clear what the other may not do without risking a military, and thus perhaps a nuclear, confrontation. Over a period of time, if the deterrence strategy is convincing, these proscriptions become incorporated into the pattern of their subsystemic interaction. But among nuclear superpowers, a set of mutually respected proscriptions on certain kinds of conduct cannot be achieved except if the proscriptions are accepted by both sides. This in effect means that the system of proscription must be perceived as mutually advantageous at least in its application over a longer period of time, if not in each single encounter. A way to achieve this is to articulate the set of proscriptions, utilizing principles which are reciprocally applicable to both sides. Reciprocity is, therefore, key to creating the mutuality of benefit essential to the building of a conventionally respected pattern of behavior in the superpower subsystem.

Reciprocity is also essential to making credible a nation's commitment to a deterrence norm in any particular confrontation. In any encounter between the United States and the Soviet Union in which deterrence strategy is to be invoked to prevent the

1. *The Strategy of Conflict,* p. 13.

Russians from taking an initiative we are not prepared to tolerate, the Soviet leaders must be convinced that their U.S. counterparts really would, if necessary, resort to preventive force. The credibility of a deterrence strategy in any particular superpower confrontation depends upon military capability plus commitment. These two ingredients, although related, are also significantly independent of each other. Thus, for example, the Soviets perceived us to have military capability with which to meet their invasion of Czechoslovakia but little or no commitment to use it. They proved to be right. But it is never easy to manifest a commitment in a way persuasive to the other side. Stating an intention is not enough. Neither is mere saber-rattling. As Schelling notes, "the hardest part is communicating our own intentions." [2] The most effective way to make manifest a commitment to deter, and thus to have an effective deterrence strategy, is for the state to conduct its foreign policy in consistent accord with certain enunciated, reciprocal principles even when, in a single encounter, it is not necessarily to its short-run advantage to do so. On the other hand, the credibility of a deterrence strategy is undermined whenever the United States, in a single encounter, pursues a short-term strategy that violates its own proscriptive norms. Principled abstinence or self-denial by a superpower in an encounter with its opponent is perhaps the strongest evidence of that superpower's commitment to use force if necessary to enforce the same proscriptions against its rival.

"Deterrence," Thomas Milburn says, "is a policy that involves influencing the behavior of the other, rather than destroying him and risking destruction in return. Deterrence is not really a military concept"; it is, rather, psychological and perceptual in nature involving the creation of certain credible expectations. [3]

The credibility of our intention to deter the Soviets from tak-

---

2. *Arms and Influence,* p. 35.
3. Thomas W. Milburn, "The Concept of Deterrence: Some Logical and Psychological Considerations," 17 *Journal of Social Issues* (1951), No. 3, p. 3. (Italics omitted.)

ing certain initiatives can only be built up through a painstaking strategy of signals, usually emitted consistently over a period of time, by which we try to ensure a mutuality of expectations, a shared prediction that if Russia does X, then the United States will do Y. In a deterrence equation, Y must stand for a consequence more deleterious to Russia's interests than X is likely to be beneficial. Since a consequence so deleterious to Russia will probably also be to some extent deleterious to us, it is necessary to convince Russia that we regard Y as less deleterious than X. To deter Russia from doing X it is therefore necessary for the United States to establish credible values that so strongly resist consequence X as to lead to the conclusion that we would certainly or probably respond to X by doing Y despite the predictable cost to us. Credibility, therefore, is the *sine qua non* of deterrence strategy. Virtually no *thing* is worth the risk of total mutual destruction, and this is as apparent to an opponent as to oneself. If an enemy is to believe that you might be willing to see everything destroyed rather than lose any particular thing, he must be persuaded that your commitment is not only to a piece of territory, a resource, or some similar object but to a principle, a concept, so that in the very marrow of your existence you would risk everything to maintain it intact.

Commitment to a course of action is thus an essential ingredient in a superpower's deterrence credibility. The actual size of military establishments of states in confrontation may by itself be less important, especially among superpowers at nuclear parity, than the extent of each side's willingness to resort to force and the extent to which the other side had been made to believe that willingness.

Thus, will and the perception of will constitute an important strategic factor. While this has to some extent always been true, it is now more true than ever. In the age of nuclear balance of terror, crises among the great powers juxtapose disputants, each of which has the ultimate power not to win but to deny victory to the other. If, therefore, an actual victory is nevertheless won in a critical confrontation, it is likely to be because one side persuaded the other to let it win. Persuasion in these instances invariably involves military-tactical factors, but most of all it involves psychological ones—factors that permit the initiator state to persuade its opponent that it is not worth the price necessary to deny the initiator his objective. So, too, if a victory is denied without recourse to the ultimate weapons of mutual destruction, it will be because the respondent persuaded the initiator that it was not worth the price necessary to pursue the initiative. Again, as Henry Kissinger points out, "deterrence above all depends on psychological criteria." [4]

An important psychological factor reinforcing the will to act is a nation's knowledge that its initiative is consistent with the prevailing systemic pattern of conduct, that is to say, in conformity with precedent. Equally, the belief that an opponent is acting in accordance with principles one has oneself devised and from which one has previously benefited, undermines the will to resist the opponent's initiative.

Take the case of a highly secret warplane flown by a defecting pilot of state *B* to an airport in state *A*. *B* requests the immediate return of the airplane. Much of the press and public of state *A* demand that the plane be kept and its secrets studied, but the leaders of *A* return it to *B,* stating that they are acting on the basis of established norms of international conduct. A few weeks later, a state-*A* pilot flies an equally secret airplane to *B*. The leaders of *B* would be in little doubt as to the credibility of threats by *A*'s leaders to use force if necessary to recover the craft. The leaders of *A* would be seen to have mortgaged their options, to have made themselves hostages to their earlier principled conduct. To survive politically, they would need to secure the return of their airplane, by force if necessary. The reciprocal application of a systemic norm to a state's own disadvantage thus makes credible, as no other psychological device can, its will to deter its

4.   Henry M. Kissinger, *American Foreign Policy: Three Essays,* New York: W. W. Norton, 1969, p. 61.

opponent from violating the same norm. Conversely, the failure of a state to apply a reciprocal norm to its own disadvantage lowers the credibility of its will to deter others from violating that norm. If state A had kept the airplane, asserting that it had a right to do so, then its subsequent threats to use force against state B if necessary to secure the release of its own craft would probably carry less credibility.

Any commitment to a policy of deterrence becomes manifestly less credible if the deterring superpower fails to deter itself from doing the kinds of things it seeks to prevent its opponent doing. In this strategic sense, to be credible, deterrence must also be reciprocal. This is quite aside from the systemic, social, and moral implications of reciprocity. The Cuban missile crisis offers an opportunity for speculative application of this theory. Although it has generally been treated as a completely successful instance of U.S. strategic planning, the very fact that the crisis arose at all must be seen as a failure of deterrence, and was so treated by President Kennedy. As Seyom Brown notes, "Kennedy had been insisting publicly that the United States could not allow Cuba to become a base for Soviet 'offensive' weapons. It was as much the fact of this drawing of the line in public as it was the actual military situation created by the Soviet deployments that underlay Kennedy's definition of the deployment as intolerable." [5] Why did the Soviets nevertheless persist? Why did the President's warnings fail to carry credibility? It is at least possible that the Soviets did not expect the United States to cross the brink of war to force the removal of Russian missiles from Cuba so long as American missiles continued to be stationed in Turkey.

Robert Kennedy and Roger Hilsman [6] have both indicated that at the beginning of his administration the President had ordered the evacuation of the Turkish missiles and had entered the Cuban missile crisis believing the order to have been carried out.

5. Brown, *op. cit.*, 1968, p. 259.
6. Robert Kennedy, *op. cit.*; Roger Hilsman, *To Move a Nation* (New York: Dell Publishing Co., 1968).

It appears that he was furious to discover the missiles were still in place. It is interesting to speculate what might have happened had Kennedy known the facts somewhat earlier, before the crisis arose. Had the warning against the installation of Soviet missiles in Cuba been coupled with the enunciation of a reciprocal proscriptive norm, had that norm been applied by the United States against itself, and had our missiles been publicly withdrawn from Turkey, would the Soviets have been deterred and the crisis averted? Certainly the credibility of the President's warnings would have been enhanced. It would have been apparent to an inveterate politician like Khrushchev that Kennedy meant business and was staking his career on the reciprocal proscriptive principle. Moreover, it would have been clear that the United States was offering Russia a reciprocal principle with reciprocal benefits and not merely a unilateral threat with all the costs on one side and the benefits on the other. As Thomas Milburn has said, "One would ordinarily expect that he could change the direction of behavior of another more effectively, not alone by blocking the other's subjective probability of achieving success in one direction, but by increasing the subjective probability for success, and even its meaning, for taking some other path or direction." [7]

It takes consistency of strategic conduct over a period of time to develop a proscriptive norm of mutually reciprocal application and to make credible a state's commitment to it. It is conceivable that the United States, had it decided early enough and manifested its decision with strategic consistency over a period of years, could have evolved a policy of deterrence which would have prevented the Soviets from risking an invasion of Czechoslovakia in 1968. How might this have been accomplished? Again, verbal strategy is of crucial importance. When Chairman Khrushchev proclaimed his policy of "many roads to socialism" and went to some lengths to reassure President Tito of Yugoslavia and the leaders of other socialist states of their right to sovereign control over their own

7.   Milburn, *loc. cit.*, p. 8.

destinies, the United States might have seized this opportunity to establish its commitment to a world system in which national sovereignty and especially territorial inviolability was the cardinal principle.

Such a commitment could have been made credible over a period of time by a series of high-level statements in which the prestige of the United States, especially that of the office of its President, was unequivocally "laid on the line" in support of a policy of national sovereignty in such a way that the Soviet leaders would have known that the United States could permit Russia to invade an independent state only at the cost of being publicly discredited. As Schelling states, what is required in shaping a credible instance of deterrence is "to get ourselves into a position where we cannot fail to react as we said we would—where we just cannot help it—or where we would be obliged by some overwhelming cost of not reacting in the manner we had declared." [8] A state can get itself into this "hostage" position by some token military commitment; the allied forces in Berlin serve just this purpose. Or it can achieve a similar result by publicly staking its national prestige, its ideology, or its principles. It was this which President Kennedy was trying to do in warning Russia before the Soviet missiles were installed that he would not under any circumstances tolerate the stationing of "offensive" missiles in Cuba. A comparably firm verbal commitment by the United States, frequently reiterated, to a global system barring direct military intervention by any superpower in any sovereign state for any reason whatsoever would have accorded with Soviet policy assertions in the period of de-Stalinization, would have underscored the norms of the U.N. Charter, and would clearly have had the support of most small and virtually all the nonaligned states. Had we asserted such a policy over a number of years, its systemic normativity would have been reinforced as would the credibility of our commitment to it.

The credibility of such an asserted policy would further have

8.   *Arms and Influence*, p. 43.

been enhanced had the United States reciprocally imposed this policy upon itself, even to its own short-run disadvantage. The extensively deliberated decision by the Kennedy Administration not to invade Cuba could have been proclaimed a dramatic instance of our consistent and high-priority adherence to the principle of respecting all national territorial integrity without exception. Had the United States not sent its forces into the Dominican Republic and publicly forsworn military intervention, then the credibility of our commitment to the proscriptive norm would by 1968 have taken on the persuasive force of what Schelling calls a "tradition." [9] It would have been strategically dangerous, at the very least, for the Soviets to ignore and ride roughshod over such a long-standing tradition of U.S. foreign policy. Conversely, since we had not developed a credible, long-standing commitment to a proscriptive norm applicable to the Czechoslovak crisis, it would have been highly dangerous for the United States in August of 1968 suddenly to have tried to deter the Soviet invasion.

The credibility of a deterrence policy is thus enhanced when the deterring state applies and verbally proclaims the application of the policy not only against the state it seeks to deter, but also against its own interests. By denying itself a gain which it could have had, the deterring state heightens its manifest investment in the policy, which makes it patently more difficult to retreat from its commitment in a subsequent confrontation with an opponent. Conversely, a commitment to a policy of deterrence becomes much less credible if the deterring state fails to deter itself from doing the kinds of things it seeks to prevent its opponent from doing. In this sense, to be credible, deterrence must also be reciprocal.

In devising a credible deterrence concept, the verbal strategist must also ensure that words uttered in enunciating the proscriptive principle are clear and of the highest range of intentionality, that we say what we mean and mean what we say. As Thomas Schelling has shown, what state *A* can get away with in a crisis depends in part on the expectations it shares with its op-

9. *The Strategy of Conflict,* p. 106.

ponent, state *B,* as to what state *B*'s reaction will be. But *A*'s guess as to what *B* will do takes into account not only what *B* actually thinks about *A*'s act, but what *B* thinks that *A* thinks that *B* thinks, where, in other words, their expectations intersect. To illustrate: Suppose *A* and *B* are boarding-school roommates. At supper, sponge cake is served for dessert and *A* passes his helping to *B,* saying "I hate that stuff." The next evening chocolate cake is served and, as *A* momentarily looks away, *B* digs into *A*'s helping. "But you said yesterday you hated that stuff," *B* explains, de- priving *A* of a clear-cut issue on which to fight, perhaps even causing him to hesitate until after the cake has been consumed. In this situation *B* may have been reasonably sure that *A* had not meant to include chocolate cake with sponge cake in the category of "that stuff," but *B* will also know that *A* has reasonable grounds to believe that *B,* because of *A*'s inexact verbal behavior, really expected chocolate cake to be in the category of "that stuff." Thus *A* and *B* share the expectation that *A* believes that *B* believes that *A* believes, etc., that chocolate cake is "in." This obviously gives *B* an advantage when it comes to a potential crisis over *A*'s cake, because *A* can act against *B* only with force, at the cost of seeming dangerously churlish and erratic, and only by an assault on the system of honoring shared expectations that makes tolerable *A*'s and *B*'s rooming together.

As we have seen, systemic interaction in the international community depends upon the operation of a fundamental, norma- tive principle of reciprocity. But in a world of cultural, political, and ethical diversity, reciprocity is no automatic mechanism. Each interaction between states, if it is to reinforce rather than weaken the system, must therefore give rise not merely to a reciprocal right but to mutually shared expectations about the range of equivalent interactions to which the right will and will *not* apply. Verbal behavior can play an important role in the creation of these genuinely shared expectations, in clarifying what is "in" and what is "out." But by the same token, a state's verbal behavior can confuse, mislead, and obfuscate not only the listeners' but the speaker's expectations.

The classic case is the speech made by Secretary of State Dean Acheson on January 12, 1950, to the National Press Club, in Washington, D.C. In this address, Acheson defined a "defensive perimeter" that ran "from the Ryukyus to the Philippines." He included defense guarantees specifically to Japan and the Philippines and implicitly to the states lying on the U.S. side of this perimeter.[10] Although the primary audience was in Washington, the secondary audience was obviously the nations of Asia and the world. What made the speech historically notable was its omission of South Korea from the ambit of the perimeter and the subsequent invasion of the Republic of Korea by North Korea in the fall of the same year. Of course, it cannot be proven that this omission was the signal North Korea decided to act on, but it is evidently true that U.S. policy failed to deter North Korea and that the Acheson speech did nothing to communicate to the enemy our willingness to fight to deny him his goal. The Acheson speech failed to achieve what Schelling calls a "coordination of expectations." [11]

All verbal behavior by persons speaking for the state in the context of systemic hostility must be planned with a conscious awareness of the implications of words as signals of our intentionality. All purposive signaling thus involves an element of "bargaining" [12] as well as of "prediction." [13] Through its verbal strategy a state should propose to its opponent the parameters of their future interaction, and it should do so in such a way as to make its adherence to those parameters clear, credible and, if possible, tolerable to the other side.

10. Dean Acheson, "Crisis in Asia—An Examination of U.S. Policy." United States, Department of State, *Bulletin,* XXII, Jan. 23, 1950, p. 116.
11. *The Strategy of Conflict,* p. 73*ff.*
12. *Ibid.*
13. *Arms and Influence,* p. 53.

THE VERBAL STRATEGY OF COOPERATION:
THE NIXON DOCTRINE

A strategy of cooperation is one which has as its aim the initiation of an upward spiral in any ongoing systemic interaction. This can take the form of a treaty mutually transforming unregulated competitive behavior into regulated cooperation as in the test-ban and outer-space agreements or it can take the form of an agreement to set up an organizational framework for problem solving, such as the United Nations or the International Atomic Energy Agency. But the upward spiral need not begin with anything as formal as a treaty or an organization. It can sometimes be initiated by a unilateral gesture of friendship, or even by a friendly speech of a head of state.

Such gestures, particularly when articulated effectively, can be a kind of offer to the other side. In any event, policy initiatives by a nuclear superpower that affect the interests of the other superpower must always be seen in the context of mutual nuclear deterrence and thus in terms of an offer. The rival superpower needs to be persuaded to accept the offer, either by securing its active agreement or, at least, by persuading it not to use its undoubted ultimate capacity to prevent or nullify the initiative.

As with initiatives that start or reinforce a downward spiral, so initiatives intended to make the spiral turn upward can be understood by analogy to the offer-acceptance notion of contract. Any initiative by a superpower vis-à-vis the other superpower is inevitably tentative insofar as the initiator must act in the knowledge that his initiative could be nullified by failure of the rival superpower to accept it. If the initiative is part of a strategy of hostility it can be nullified, as we have seen, by the opponent's determination, whatever the risk of mutual destruction, to deter or reverse the initiative. If the initiative is part of a strategy of cooperation it can be nullified by the opponent's failure to understand the initiative's cooperative intent. If the benefits to the opponent superpower are not clearly communicated by the initiating superpower, there is unlikely to be any reciprocation and the spiral will not even complete its first circle.

However, the offer-acceptance analogy should not be pressed too far. In contract (or treaty) bargaining, a rejected offer may nevertheless be a step toward agreement. But if a superpower takes a unilateral cooperative initiative that is rejected or spurned by the other superpower, the relationship between the powers may thereby become more hostile even though, or because, the spurned initiative was intended as a step toward greater cooperation. The rejection by Stalinist Russia of the Baruch proposal for international control of nuclear weaponry at a time when the West had a nuclear monopoly profoundly affected U.S.-Soviet relations and was an element in the development of a hardened cynicism in Washington toward all subsequent Soviet arms-control proposals.[14] In efforts to improve cooperation it is sometimes better not to initiate at all than to initiate and be spurned.

If, therefore, the United States were to decide to initiate a transformation of its systemic relationship with the Soviet Union to replace the hostile strategy of the Johnson and Brezhnev doctrines with a more cooperative norm, one that would give greater national freedom to the smaller states within each superpower's region, then our initiatives would have to be designed to be reciprocated if possible and to do little damage if they are not. Hypothetically the United States could offer Russia a full-blown treaty incorporating a new code of conduct respecting national sovereignty and self-determination, restating the neglected U.N. Charter rules pertaining to nonintervention and harkening back to the Khrushchev doctrines of "sovereign equality" and the "many roads to socialism." But given the present state of U.S.-Soviet relations, Russia is as unlikely to accept such an offer as we are to make it. Before such a significant change in the normative rules of inter-

14. Cf., Harry S Truman, *Memoirs*, II, *Years of Trial and Hope*, Garden City, N.Y.: Doubleday & Co., 1956, pp. 10–11.

action between the superpowers could ever come about, a very large number of smaller steps would have to be taken, steps designed to lead gradually, incrementally, toward an eventual reorientation of subsystemic norms.

Let us assume that the United States has decided on a campaign to achieve a normative reorientation that would repeal the Johnson and Brezhnev doctrines. Such a campaign can be conceived in terms of a series of steps proceeding through four phases. The first step would be exceedingly small. Subsequent steps, if reciprocated, would become consecutively larger. The four phases are:

1. change in climate
2. change in images
3. change in concrete conduct
4. change in systemic norms of conduct.

In each of these phases verbal behavior plays an important role. In the early initiatory phases, that role becomes preeminent and requires the most careful strategic planning.

When President Johnson and Premier Kosygin consciously sought through communiqués and statements to engender "the spirit of Glassboro," they did so because they hoped that a new climate or mood shared by their two nations could help reshape the pattern of interaction between them. This was an instance of verbal and other strategic behavior being planned and used to alter and strengthen the subsystemic pattern of interaction between the United States and Russia by first inducing *climatic* change (phase 1). The wartime speeches of Churchill and Roosevelt did much to help create that hardiest of climates, the "special relationship" between Britain and the United States. Churchill's Fulton, Missouri, speech is widely credited with a share in transforming the climate of wartime superpower cooperation, which in turn ushered in the new systemic patterns of the cold war. These speeches played a part in changing the way countries felt about each other. Climate is a shared way of feeling between two or more states which persists over a prolonged period of time. During its persistence, states tend to develop a high level of mutually shared expectations and of patterned, systemic conduct responsive to those expectations. If the climate is one of growing friendliness, the patterns of interaction tend to become cooperative, as after Glassboro. Whether the climatic change is toward conducing systematic friendliness and cooperation or toward a pattern of organized hostility is a high question of national policy which ought to be resolved by deliberate, planned, purposeful choice and executed by a similarly deliberate rational strategy.

If climate has to do with feeling, image has to do with the way one state sees another. Boulding defines image as the "total cognitive, affective, and evaluative structure of the behavior unit, or its internal view of itself and its universe." [15] For our purposes, it is used simply to denote the way a state "sees" other specific actors in the international arena. Thus, an image is usually a set of collective attributes that one state perceives in another. These ways of seeing states have been extensively studied. One authority reports that a study of Soviet attitudes in 1960 indicated a perception of the United States as "threatening," [16] "aggressive," ruled by "capitalist circles," and "exploitative." [17] During the same period the United States was found by another study to be seeing Russia as "simply making a power play for extended and perhaps global control. . . ." [18] Everyone to some extent anthropomorphizes his own and other states; images are a manifestation of this reification. Images may not always yield valid data about the perceived state, but are valid and important data about the perceiver, whose conduct can frequently be understood and even predicted by understanding his images, his "realities." [19] The way

15. Kenneth E. Boulding, "National Images and International Systems," in Rosenau, *op. cit.,* p. 423.
16. Ralph K. White, "Images in the Context of International Conflict: Soviet Perceptions of the U.S. and the U.S.S.R." in Kelman, *op. cit.,* p. 244.
17. *Ibid.,* p. 254.
18. S. B. Whitey, "Public Opinion on War and Shelters," *New University Thought,* 1962, 2(3), pp. 6–19.
19. Cf., Joseph H. de Rivera, *The Psychological Dimension of Foreign Policy,* Columbus, Ohio: Charles E. Merrill, 1968, esp. chapter 2, "The Construction of Reality," pp. 19–64.

two states "see" each other will frequently affect the way they interact. A pattern of systemic cooperation is not likely to develop between states that perceive each other as evil, aggressive, and immoral. Thus image transformation is a step toward systemic change and development of cooperative patterns of interaction.

Image and climate are significantly different, if related, concepts. Image is a way of seeing the other, while climate is a way of feeling toward the other. Image is rarely a shared experience while climate cannot be anything else. If there is to be a climate of interaction, the way state *A* feels toward *B* must coincide with the way *B* feels toward *A*. But state *A* can sustain an image of *B* which does not in the least resemble *B*'s image of *A*. Images are not nearly as reciprocally dependent as is climate. State *A*'s way of seeing *B* is rarely based on *B*'s way of seeing *A;* most Americans scarcely know the Soviet image of their country. But *A*'s way of feeling about *B* is usually to some extent dependent on, and conditioned by, *B*'s way of feeling toward *A*. This is probably because we usually know or think we know how another state feels toward us, but we know we have little idea of how it sees us. States sometimes communicate their feelings but rarely their images. The same holds for interpersonal relations. We frequently know or believe we know how others feel about us and that affects our way of feeling towards them. But we hope in vain, with Robert Burns, "O wad some Pow'r the giftie gie us, To see oursels as others see us!"

Image and climate, related but different, do affect each other. A climate developing between states may confirm, suspend, contradict, ignore, or alter the images the parties have of each other. Conversely, when two states do happen to see each other in similar or compatible images a friendly climate is likely to develop.

From the point of view of system building and system transformation, climate, because of its mutuality, is the more important concept. Lasswell points out that a climatic mood, being mutually shared by two or more actors, connotes a situation in which international behavior is marked by "relatively stable occurrences" [20] and shared "expectations about past, present and future occurrences. . . ." [21] Climate is thus a condition which, sustained over a period of time, conduces to the development of consistent patterns of interaction, whether cooperative or hostile.

Both *images* and *climate* have been studied in terms of their resistance to change. Professor Etzioni [22] has shown empirically that climate is relatively susceptible to change, while the work by Janus and Smith on images emphasizes that "attempts at producing changes in social or political prejudices and stereotypes," key ingredients of hostile images, "generally meet with an extraordinarily high degree of psychological resistance. . . ." [23] and are thus much harder to transform. It appears, however, that a change in international climate, if sustained, can gradually promote a change in image. As another authority puts it "people individually or collectively, view the occurrence of events in a perspective formed as much by a prevailing climate or trend of opinion as by their past experiences and perceptions." [24] Initially in a period of thaw, the popular attitude appears to be, "Well, the other side may be evil, but at least they want to work with us." But if "they" continue to work with "us" over a number of different issues and a prolonged period of time, even the image of "them" as evil may give way to some more accommodating perceptive set.

How a strategy of climate transformation was planned, executed, and brought to fruition is ably examined in Etzioni's study "The Kennedy Experiment." [25] Etzioni found that the "vicious

20. Harold D. Lasswell, "The Climate of International Action," in Kelman, *op. cit.*, p. 340.
21. *Ibid.*
22. Amitai Etzioni, "The Kennedy Experiment," *The Western Political Science Quarterly*, XX, 2, Part 1, June 1967, pp. 361*ff.*
23. Irving L. Janus and M. Brewster Smith, "Effects of Education and Persuasion on National and International Images" in Kelman, *op. cit.*, p. 195.
24. Karl W. Deutsch and Richard L. Merritt, "Effects of Events on National and International Images," *ibid.*, p. 151.
25. Etzioni, *supra*, n. 22.

circle of hostile moves and counter-moves" was broken by a kind of technique in which one state communicates to the other a small, unilateral indication of friendliness. He compared this to "psychoanalytic technique—increased and improved communication" conveying "a friendlier state of mind." [26] Since these first gestures must be taken against an established mutual pattern of hostility and since the first gesture in this "therapy" must be unilateral, it is not likely to involve important economic, military, or political concessions. But Etzioni's study showed that the psychological significance of a very small, largely symbolic act could be substantially enhanced by a verbal strategy carefully conceived for that purpose. President Kennedy's speech at American University on June 10, 1963, emphasized the futility of war and took a particularly conciliatory tone. Etzioni points out that the speech "set the *context* for the unilateral initiatives to follow." [27]

The actual initiative announced in the speech was the cessation of all nuclear tests in the atmosphere on the condition that other countries did the same. Etzioni notes that this "was basically a psychological gesture and not a unilateral arms limitation step" because the United States was far ahead of the Soviet Union in deliverable nuclear capability and had recently conducted a large round of tests yielding data that would take one to two years of processing.[28] What transformed this small gesture into a psychologically significant unilateral initiative was the President's verbal strategy. His speech made it clear to the Russians that a test pause was but the first small bid in a deliberately conceived plan for altering the whole climate of U.S.-Soviet interaction. The strategic role of words and concepts here is to give definition to mute acts. Any "concrete measure," in Etzioni's words, "can be interpreted in a variety of ways" and thus "it is necessary to spell out the general state of mind these steps attempt to communicate." [29]

26. *Ibid.*, p. 362.
27. *Ibid.*, p. 365.
28. *Ibid.*
29. *Ibid.*

Although, as we have noted, country *A* must always expect country *B* to take advantage of the reciprocal equivalent of any downward spiral in the level of systemic interaction which *A* may initiate, it cannot be equally certain of reciprocity in initiating an upward spiral. Here a delicate and subtle bargaining is likely to occur, analogous to the Kula exchange observed by Malinowski:

> . . . the Kula exchange has always to be a *gift*, followed by a *counter-gift;* it can never be a barter, a direct exchange with assessment of equivalents and with haggling. There must be always in the Kula two transactions, distinct in name, in nature and in time. The exchange is opened by an initial or opening gift called *vaga*, and closed by a final or return present called *yotile*. They are both ceremonial gifts, they have to be accompanied by the blow of a conch shell, and the present is given ostentatiously and in public. The native term "to throw" a valuable describes well the nature of the act. For, though the valuable has to be handed over by the giver, the receiver hardly takes any notice of it, and seldom receives it actually into his hands. The etiquette of the transaction requires that the gift should be given in an off-hand, abrupt, almost angry manner, and received with equivalent nonchalance and disdain.[30]

Strategically planned verbal behavior is designed by the giver to enhance the apparent value to the receiver of an initiating offer or "gift," the real cost of which must be kept as low as possible to the giver at this inceptive stage. In other words, the object of a verbal strategy of cooperation in this phase is to make the initiator's gesture worth far more to one's opponent than its actual cost to oneself.

For example, as the revolutionary junta of Peru or the elected socialist government of Chile embark on a leftist course of eco-

---

30. Bronislaw Malinowski, *Argonauts of the Western Pacific: An Account of Native Enterprise and Adventure in the Archipelagoes of Melanesian New Guinea,* London: Routledge & Kegan Paul, Ltd., New York: E. P. Dutton, p. 532. From a chapter entitled "The Kula in Dobu-Technicalities of the Exchange."

nomic change, nationalizing U.S.-owned industry and moving toward a socialist society, the United States will have an opportunity to begin to move away from the Johnson Doctrine one step at a time, pausing between steps to see whether there is any comparable tendency on the part of Moscow to modify the Brezhnev Doctrine. We can begin by stating unequivocally, even while pressing our demands for compensation, that on no account will military force be used to interfere with Peruvian or Chilean sovereignty so long as no other superpower establishes its military presence on Peruvian or Chilean soil. It has already been quite clear to most Americans for some time, despite the overreach of the Johnson Doctrine, that we would be extremely unlikely to try to remove a socialist government of Peru or Chile by military force. It is probably far less clear, however, to the rest of the region—for example, to Peru or Chile. Nor is it clear to the Soviets. A ringing affirmation of Peru's or Chile's right to go its own way, however well- or ill-advised that way may be, so long as it does not serve as a base for a foreign state or for the subversion of other states in the hemisphere, would be a highly significant and credible initiating gesture in any strategy to alter the climate of the Johnson-Brezhnev era. It would also put the ball in Moscow's court.

A significant beginning in this direction has already been made by President Nixon. In his foreign affairs message to Congress of February 18, 1970,[31] he put the United States position vis-à-vis the Americas rather differently from the Johnson Doctrine:

> Within the broad commonality of our relationship, there is great diversity. In a period of such profound social and cultural change emerging domestic structures will differ by country, reflecting various historical roots, particular contexts and national priorities. We can anticipate different inter-

31. "United States Foreign Policy for the 1970's: A New Strategy for Peace" in *The New York Times*, Feb. 19, 1970, pp. 19C–30C at pp. 21C–22C; contains specific reference to the propositions of the Nixon Doctrine.

pretations of reality, different conceptions of self-interest and different conclusions on how to resolve problems.

The United States must comprehend these phenomena. We must recognize national interests may indeed diverge from ours rather than merge.

In an obvious reference to the Johnson Doctrine, Nixon declared, "Our power overshadowed the formal relationship of equality and even our restrained use of this power was not wholly reassuring. As a result, tension between us grew."

On January 4, 1971, in the televised discussion with network correspondents, the President went further. Although noting in reference to Chile that "what happened is not something that we welcome," the President made it clear that "for the United States to have intervened, intervened in a free election and to have turned it around, I think would have had repercussions all over Latin America that would have been far worse than what has happened in Chile. . . . We recognized the right of any country to have internal policies and an internal government quite different from what we might approve of. What we [are] interested in [is] their policy towards us in the foreign policy field." [32]

This appears to indicate a well-calculated attempt to alter our verbal and conceptual strategy vis-à-vis Latin America. It seems also to be a beginning of a deliberate effort to alter America's image and the climate of international relations. This effort is characterized above all by the Nixon Doctrine,[33] which sets a theme developed by Secretary Rogers in relation to Latin America, a determination on our part to "be less intrusive and less domineering. We can speak with a less strident voice," he noted, particularly "by conducting our international affairs with a bit more modesty. . . ." [34] This could well be followed by a more specific gesture

32. *The New York Times,* Jan. 6, 1971, p. 42.
33. Cf., President Nixon's address to the Nation on Nov. 3, 1969. United States, Department of State, *Bulletin,* LXI, No. 1587, Nov. 24, 1969, p. 437.
34. Secretary of State Rogers' address before the Department of State's national foreign policy conference for editors and broadcasters on

manifesting our intention. If the gesture is not thereafter reciprocated by some comparable Soviet retreat, at least verbally, from the most extreme assertions of the Brezhnev Doctrine—a reassurance, for example, to Yugoslavia—the gesture would have cost us nothing, since no course of action would have been taken which we would not have pursued in any case.

But the Soviets might reciprocate. Etzioni has shown, for example, that in every instance President Kennedy's gestures were in fact reciprocated. The "Russians responded not just by reciprocating American initiatives but by offering some initiatives of their own" [35] and "for each move that was made, the Soviets reciprocated." [36] There is some reason to hope that such reciprocation would also follow a small, concrete U.S. initiative to back away from the Johnson-Brezhnev doctrines; the Soviets, too, could conceivably be beginning to feel embarrassed by the constant pointed reminders of their fraternal leaders, such as President Ceaucescu, that solidarity and mutual aid presupposes relations of equality, that no country has the right to interfere in the affairs of others and that when such interference occurs, it greatly prejudices socialism at large.[37] "By the world socialist system we understand not a bloc," they are saying, "in which the states are fused into a whole, giving up their national sovereignty, but the assertion of Socialism as an international force by its victory in several independent states, which develop independently. . . ." [38] The assertions are not very different from those of leading Latin-American democracies in response to the Johnson Doctrine.

With such rebukes stinging their ears, both the United States and the Soviet Union are already at present stopping short of a

Jan. 15. United States, Department of State, *Bulletin,* LXII, No. 1597, Feb. 2, 1970, p. 118.

35. Etzioni, *loc. cit.,* p. 369.
36. *Ibid.,* p. 368.
37. President Ceaucescu of Romania, opening the Quadrennial Congress of the Romanian Communist Party, *The Times* of London, Aug. 7, 1969, p. 3.
38. President Ceaucescu, Quadrennial Romanian Party Congress, *International Herald Tribune,* Aug. 7, 1969, p. 2.

rigid, consistent application of the Johnson-Brezhnev doctrines to their respective regions. The United States has not invaded Cuba, Peru, or Chile; the Soviets have not attacked Romania, Yugoslavia, or Albania. What is at first needed to initiate a change in climate leading to the eventual repeal of these norms is not a radical shift in actual conduct but a formulation by each state of its verbal behavior so as to emphasize the limitations it is already imposing on its asserted doctrine. President Nixon has already declared that in hemispheric relations the goal "should be to create a community of independent, self-reliant states linked together in a vital and useful association." In such a free association, "the United States should contribute, not dominate" and "each nation must be true to its own character." He visualized "a partnership in which all voices are heard and none is predominant." [39] Developing further this new conceptualization of inter-American relations, the President indicated a willingness to relax the two-ghetto subsystem and a preference for a new conceptual basis for relations between a superpower and smaller neighbors:

> In a period of such profound social and cultural change, emerging domestic structures will differ by country, reflecting various historical roots, particular contexts, and national priorities. We can anticipate different interpretations of reality, different conceptions of self-interest and different conclusions on how to resolve problems.
>
> The United States must comprehend these phenomena. We must recognize national interests may indeed diverge from ours rather than merge. Our joint task is to construct a community of institutions and interests broad and resilient enough to accommodate our national divergencies. [40]

These modifications of the Johnson Doctrine—the change of emphasis from superpower enforcement of political regimen-

39. U.S. Foreign Policy for the 1970's: A New Strategy for Peace; A Report to the Congress, by President Richard M. Nixon, February 18, 1970. United States, Department of State, *Bulletin*, LXII, No. 1602, March 9, 1970, p. 290.
40. *Ibid.*, p. 293.

tation to a permissive, if tentative, attitude toward political varie-
gation among the states of the region—are the essence of the
Latin-American version of the Nixon Doctrine. What induced the
shift is not, however, explicable solely by a change in management
at the top of the U.S. government. Much else has changed in the
United States since 1965. The failure to win in Vietnam despite
vast expenditures of men and resources and the disintegration of
social myths that had previously held in check the social and
economic expectations of America's lower classes have compelled a
rethinking of national priorities and goals. Washington has had no
choice but to respond to a massive demand from U.S. citizens
to reverse the decay of cities, the pollution of the environment, and
the inaccessibility of health services. At the same time, taxation
has approached the upper reaches of profitability. Perhaps most
important of all, new values and a new personal definition among
the young has made a large segment of the population unresponsive
to the traditional vicarious satisfactions hitherto derived from
national aggrandizement, territorial expansion, and a winning global strategy.

Perhaps similar internal factors will begin, or have already
begun, to operate within the Soviet Union, albeit behind a façade of
authoritarian conformity. There are indications that Soviet finances,
too, are overextended. Russia now spends five times as much as
the United States supporting its client states in the Middle East.
Large expenditures are being made in North Vietnam and Cuba.
Further demands for aid of unknown but undoubtedly large scale
will be made by Peru, Chile, and several other states in Latin
America and Africa—all for results the significance of which is
not readily apparent to the Moscow man in the street. Meanwhile,
poor harvests, lagging industrial production, and a failure not only
to catch up to the American standard of living but to stay abreast
even of Japan's, is beginning to have its effect not only on
Soviet intellectuals but also on scientists and technocrats who
may hitherto have been willing to tolerate a closed society on
the assumption that this would conduce to rapid economic growth.

Among the young, there is an awareness of student and youth movements in the rest of the world—the new values, the new "reality." Within the Soviet Union, among ethnic minorities in particular, there is a renewed desire for self-expression. In the satellite states, the cost of supporting unpopular authoritarian regimes in Poland led to the riots of Christmas, 1970, and to the fall of Gomulka. The Soviet Union has had to subsidize the bid by Gomulka's successors to popularize themselves through new subsidies. Poland was never regarded as a stable ally of the Soviet Union. But Czechoslovakia, alone among East European nations, was. Now, as a result of the invasion, Czechoslovakia's strong economy is stagnant and even the Czechoslovaks can no longer be counted on in Moscow.

It is at least possible that a new generation of Soviet political leadership will be brought by these events to the realization that more attention must be paid to perfecting Soviet society, less to neo-imperial interventions and global influence-seeking. Russian cities, like American, are suffering from urban decay. Russian industrial pollution is endangering the environment. Russian consumers have shed old self-restraining myths and replaced them with new expectations. There are, then, profound factors operating in Soviet life to which wise politicians, even in a dictatorship, would try to be responsive. It is by no means certain that these responses to change will be forthcoming in Russia, just as it is far from clear that the Nixon Doctrine will be applied consistently in cases where the old temptations are strong. Yet the commonality of real economic, social, and political forces and factors in the Soviet Union and the United States at least encourages the hope that Moscow before long will reciprocate Washington's first small steps away from the Johnson Doctrine by some equivalent move away from the Brezhnev Doctrine. Once the reciprocal pattern, the upward spiral, is set in motion, it may have a self-reinforcing effect on internal forces in each country.

Even if the Soviet Union were not to reciprocate, and the climate were thus to remain hostile, the strategic value of the unilateral gesture would not have to be wholly lost. It can readily be *converted from a first step in a new cooperation strategy to a first step in a new strategy of deterrence.* The unilateral assertion by the United States of its determination to respect the sovereignty of small states in its region is, as we have seen, a *sine qua non* of convincing the Russians that we may in the future not be prepared to tolerate another assertion of "socialist solidarity" at the expense of a small state's national sovereignty. Both a policy of cooperation and one of deterrence can thus proceed from the same action, differentiated only by the verbal behavior which, in the case of cooperation, would place the action in a context of a larger plan for developing friendly relations and, in the case of deterrence, in a context of preventing certain unfriendly acts by our opponent. Whatever points the initiative would have failed to earn for a policy of cooperation would thus be gained for a policy of deterrence directed at the same end—the prevention of more violations of the territorial sovereignty of small states like Czechoslovakia.

If, however, President Nixon's opening initiatives are successful in eliciting reciprocal Soviet responses, a start will have been made toward changing the climate of U.S.-Soviet relations. This will be more important than the context of the gestures themselves, since the two powers at this stage will be confining themselves to small gestures of largely symbolic value. With a change in climate, however, the second phase of the strategy is reached.

Before the strategic principle of giving away "nothing for something" can be transformed into a strategy for mutual exchange of genuine valuables, a change will have to take place in the two superpowers' images of each other—not necessarily in the total spectrum of perceptive set through which the people and leaders of each see the other, but at least in those aspects of the image that directly block a genuine mutual change of policy.

Images, as we have noted, tend to be resistant to change, but an improvement in the general climate of relations may soften up the hardened stereotypes by which states that have long been caught in a downward spiral of hostility tend to perceive each other's acts and motives. The blossoming of U.S.-Soviet friendship societies and cultural exchange in times of thaw indicates the greater willingness of a society to tolerate challenges to their stereotype when the climate is one of cooperation. Leaders, in particular, can further accelerate image change because, as studies have shown, their record of public conformity to the values, norms, and perceptual images of their society tends to earn them "a fund of 'idiosyncrasy credits' that allows them to deviate with impunity when they decide to disregard one of the existing norms, which sometimes results in the entire group's shifting to a new norm." [41] Thus, the study by Janus and Smith suggests, General Eisenhower was in a position to undertake successful peace negotiations in Korea at a time "when strong norms against negotiation with the Communist adversary had created an acute crisis of policy." [42]

If, then, a change is to occur in the Johnson-Brezhnev pattern of U.S.-Soviet interaction, it is necessary first to identify those aspects of each superpower's "way of seeing" that have buttressed the pattern.

The Soviet Union invaded Czechoslovakia in the belief that the radical reforms in that country constituted a conspiracy by "the forces of internal and external reaction" to wrest Czechoslovakia away from the Eastern European security system and draw it into "the imperialist camp." Thus the reforms in Czechoslovakia appeared to Moscow as a manifestation of the expansionist "policy of ruling circles in the United States."

To Russians, the reform movement in Czechoslovakia was serving the imperial intentions of the United States. This implies an image of the Czechoslovak reformers as "agents" of the United States and West Germany and images of the United States and West Germany as imperialist nations anxious to employ the Czechoslovak reformers to Western advantage. It cannot, of course, be known whether these were the real reasons for the Soviet invasion, or whether this was really how the Kremlin per-

41. Janus and Smith, *loc. cit.,* p. 200.
42. *Ibid.*

ceived the Prague spring and the intentions of the West. But these were the reasons advanced by Soviet apologists, and they were apparently accepted by all but a tiny radical minority of the Soviet population. This indicates a perceptive set which expects and thus sees reformist elements in the satellite states to be in league with U.S.-capitalist-imperialist interests, and which expects the United States to take advantage of reformist movements in Eastern Europe in order to expand its sphere of military-imperialist hegemony to the common danger of the socialist commonwealth. Such an image of the West and of liberalizing movements has long been promoted by Soviet rhetoric. Justifying the crushing of the moderate socialist Nagy Government in Hungary in 1956, the Kremlin had even then railed against "intervention" by "international forces of reaction and counter-revolution." [43]

The United States appears to perceive radical movements within its region in almost exactly the same way. The Arbenz government of Guatemala was early branded by the State Department as an "intervention of international communism in this hemisphere." The use of force against it was thus justified in terms of hemispheric self-defense. Although no Soviet military units were ever introduced into Guatemala, it was a "given" of U.S. policy that communism is *ipso facto* an alien ideology, subservient always to Moscow's imperialist interests, and that any "activities" of an "international Communist movement" in the Western Hemisphere per se constitutes "intervention in American affairs." These activities were seen as being pursued "in the interests of an alien despotism," i.e., the Soviet Union. Our verbal strategy made it appear inconceivable that a radical leftist government in our hemisphere could be anything but an agent of Russia or that Soviet leaders would fail to use any such government to establish their

43. Ralph K. White cites a study showing that Soviet citizens "indicated a complete acceptance of official propaganda with regard to foreign affairs"; White, "Images in the Context of International Conflict: Soviet Perceptions of the U.S. and the U.S.S.R." in Kelman, *op. cit.*, p. 243.

own military-imperial hegemony. This image was widely shared by U.S. policy makers and the public.

Only in the instance of the Cuban missile crisis was there factual justification for the assertion that a radical revolutionary regime in the Western hemisphere really was leading its nation toward becoming a base for the Soviets. Nevertheless, before Soviet missiles were introduced, the United States had already branded Castro's regime as one "dominated by international Communism" and had openly called on the hemisphere to use sanctions to "prevent the establishment" of this regime and covertly tried to overthrow it by force at the Bay of Pigs. Although definitive proof is lacking, it may be contended that our refusal to distinguish between Castro's and the Kremlin's interests and our insistence that Cuba had become a captive of Soviet imperialism constituted a self-fulfilling prophecy. Whether this is so or not, the experience of Cuba did undoubtedly strengthen the U.S. image of Russia as the sponsor and exploiter of all radical revolutionary movements in the Western Hemisphere.

This image played an important part in shaping our perception of, and reaction to, the events of 1965 in the Dominican Republic. We readily justified our intervention as hemispheric self-defense against Dominican revolutionaries whom we saw as agents of an "international conspiracy" and "inspired by an outside power." There was scarcely more evidence of this in the Dominican crisis than in the Czechoslovak or Hungarian cases. Rather, as in these other instances, it was a presumption derived from passing mixed facts through the selective filter of a perceptive set. We derived our understanding of the "enemy's" actions from our image of the invariable motives and nature of "international communism."

Before any significant change in the Johnson-Brezhnev patterns of interaction can be achieved, it will be necessary for the leaders and opinion-shaping mass media of the Soviet Union and the United States in a deliberately achieved, mutually shared climate of relaxed tension to promote two crucial image changes:

1. each superpower must change its fixed a priori impressions of the nature of revolutionary or radical reform movements within its own region, and,

2. each superpower must change its fixed a priori impressions of the use made of radical movements in its region by the rival superpower.

It is well documented that many national Communist movements, both in and out of power, no longer slavishly subordinate their interests to Moscow's. Nor does Moscow invariably establish military bases or try to take over control of countries in which radical revolutionary movements gain power. There are instances and bits of evidence that reinforce the stereotype, but there is more evidence which does not. So too with the Soviet stereotype of radical reform movements in their region and our intentions to exploit them.

Studies have shown that the influence of leaders and mass media in the formulation of popular national attitudes is particularly important where foreign affairs are concerned. These "studies confirm the impression that Western publics generally, and the American public even more clearly, have kept their stated policy preferences at least loosely coordinated with the policies that they have perceived their elites as pursuing." As regards distant foreign policy issues, many persons apparently "are capable of being persuaded to accept, or at least tacitly to allow, policy innovation in previously undeveloped directions." [44] This guardedly optimistic evaluation of the prospects for image transformation depends, however, on a determined initiative by the leadership and the mass media to "take the public along."

What shape might a restructured mutual image realistically be expected to take? Any backing away from the image underlying the Johnson-Brezhnev doctrines would require Soviet and U.S. leaders to reeducate their own and the other superpower's publics to be able to make a clear distinction between, on the one hand,

44. Milton J. Rosenberg, "Images in Relation to the Policy Process: American Public Opinion on Cold-War Issues," *ibid.*, p. 305.

regimes that do not conform to the orthodox political norm in their sphere and, on the other, regimes that ally themselves militarily with the rival superpower. Such a distinction would permit the superpower to continue to employ force if necessary to prevent the establishment in its region of regimes strategically allied with a rival superpower, while excluding the use of force to prevent the establishment of genuinely national but politically deviationist regimes.

Russia, for example, seems to have been willing to make this distinction in the case of Finland and Austria, both of which are in the outskirts of Russia's security region, both of which have non-Communist regimes and essentially Western political, social, and economic institutions, but both of which cooperate with the Soviet Union to the extent of remaining strictly aloof from Western military alliances and avoiding all contact with the West that could give rise to legitimate Soviet strategic apprehensions. To some extent the United States and Cuba have, in fact but not yet in rhetoric, tentatively begun to move toward a similar "mutual accommodation." President Nixon, in particular, has been careful to link his tentative concession to radical social experimentation within Chile to an insistence that Chilean foreign policy not link that member of the hemispheric subsystem to the Soviet "family of nations." Concurrent with Nixon's assumption of a "low profile" towards Chile has gone his firm public affirmation of an "understanding" with Russia "that they would not put a military naval base into Cuba." [45] In effect, Cuba, Chile, or Peru can regard themselves as free as, but no freer than, Austria or Finland. Austria and Finland, it should however be noted, are states that have never been members of either superpower ghetto. Chile, Cuba, and Peru are all traditionally members of the U.S. sphere. It is now up to the Soviets to reciprocate by permitting nations within their traditional family also to opt for the Austrian or Finnish model. The effect of current U.S. strategy appears to be to encourage such specific

45. Transcript of the Nixon Interview with Television Correspondents, *The New York Times,* Jan. 6, 1971, p. 42.

Russian reciprocation, to lay a very tentative base for a system and strategy of partial deghettoization.

Sensing the new rules of the game in Latin America, President Allende has been insisting on his country's right to follow a Marxist economic policy and a neutralist foreign policy. But at the same time he has been at pains to reassure Washington: "we will never provide a military base that might be used against the United States. Chile will never permit her territory to be used for a military base by any foreign power—by anybody." [46] In this, the Chilean Marxist regime appears to be "accepting" the new norm of partial deghettoization for Latin America proposed by the Nixon administration. It remains to be seen whether any parallel rethinking of its relations with Eastern Europe is on the agenda of the Kremlin. In any event, for the present, the Chileans appear determined to prove that there are still "different roads to socialism" [47] and that the Chilean model would help to dissolve, rather than reinforce, the cold war image of a monolithic Moscow-dominated international communist hegemony. If they succeed, the task of deghettoization will be considerably eased.

If, then, we have decided to move the U.S.-Soviet subsystem away from its present commitment to rigid dual ghettos, our strategy will have to concern itself with a general change in the climate of subsystemic interaction, i.e., in the mood of U.S.-Soviet relations; it will next have to make a start in the slow and complex process of reshaping our long-held and much-reinforced image of *all* socialist movements as part of a monolithic, aggressive international-Communist conspiracy controlled and invariably subservient to the strategic interests of Moscow. Such a change of image can only come as part of a similar Soviet effort to amend the images that prompt them to perceive all liberalizing movements striving to make socialism more humane, national, or democratic, as part of a worldwide capitalist-imperialist conspiracy to encircle the Soviet Union and overthrow its regime.

46. *The New York Times,* March 25, 1971, p. 1.
47. *Ibid.,* p. 24.

We are at the crossroads. If they and we so choose, the Soviet Union and the United States can now move from the dual-ghetto patterns of subsystem interaction to a new norm that safeguards the superpowers' justified, essential strategic interests, while yet permitting much greater expression of the national individuality of smaller states within each superpower's region.

Index

Thomas M. Franck is Professor of International Law at the New York University Law School and Director of the Center for International Studies.

Edward Weisband is Assistant Director of the Center for International Studies and Assistant Professor of Politics at Washington Square College, New York University.

DATE DUE